INDEX

ON CENSORSHIP

INDEX ON CENSORSHIP 6 1995

Volume 24 No 6 November/December 1995   Issue 167

Editor & Chief Executive
Ursula Owen
Director of Administration
Philip Spender
Deputy Editor
Judith Vidal-Hall
Production Editor
Rose Bell
Fundraising Manager
Elizabeth Twining
News Editor
Adam Newey
Editorial Assistants
Anna Feldman
Philippa Nugent
Africa
Adewale Maja-Pearce
Eastern Europe
Irena Maryniak
Circulation & Marketing Director
Louise Tyson
Subscriptions Manager
Kelly Cornwall

Accountant
Suzanne Doyle
Volunteer Assistants
Michaela Becker
Laura Bruni
Nathalie de Broglio
Erum Faruqi
Ian Franklin
Kirsty Gordon
Joe Hipgrave
Michelle James
Claudia Jessop
Dionne King
Jenny Liebscher
Anne Logie
Nicholas McAulay
Jamie McLeish
Grazia Pelosi
Sarah Smith
Katheryn Thal
Saul Venit
Henry Vivian-Neal
Predrag Zivkovic

Directors
Louis Blom-Cooper, Ajay Chowdhury, Caroline
Moorehead, Ursula Owen, Peter Palumbo, Jim Rose,
Anthony Smith, Philip Spender, Sue Woodford (Chair)

Council
Ronald Dworkin, Amanda Foreman, Thomas
Hammarberg, Clive Hollick, Geoffrey Hosking, Michael
Ignatieff, Mark Littman, Pavel Litvinov, Robert McCrum,
Uta Ruge, William Shawcross, Suriya Wickremasinghe

Patrons
Chinua Achebe, David Astor, Robert L Bernstein, Harold
Evans, Richard Hamilton, Stuart Hampshire, Yehudi
Menuhin, Iris Murdoch, Philip Roth, Tom Stoppard,
Michael Tippett, Morris West

Australian committee
Philip Adams, Blanche d'Alpuget, Bruce Dawe,
Adele Horin, Angelo Loukakis, Ken Methold,
Laurie Muller, Robert Pullan and David Williamson c/o
Ken Methold, PO Box 6073, Toowoomba West,
Queensland 4350

Danish committee
Paul Grosen, Niels Barfoed, Claus Sønderkøge, Herbert
Pundik, Nils Thostrup, Toni Liversage and Björn
Elmquist, c/o Claus Sønderkøge, Utkaervej 7, Ejerslev,
DK-7900 Nykobing Mors

Dutch committee
Maarten Asscher, Gerlien van Dalen, Christel Jansen,
Bert Janssens, Chris Keulemans, Frank Ligtvoet, Hans
Rutten, Mineke Schipper, Steffie Stokvis, Martine Stroo
and Steven de Winter, c/o Gerlien van Dalen and Chris
Keulemans, De Balie, Kleine-Gartmanplantsoen 10, 1017
RR Amsterdam

Norwegian committee
Trond Andreassen, Jahn Otto Johansen, Alf Skjeseth and
Sigmund Strømme, c/o NFF, Skippergt. 23, 0154 Oslo

Swedish committee
Ana L Valdés and Gunilla Abrandt, c/o *Dagens Nyheter*,
Kulturredaktionen, S-105 15 Stockholm, Sweden

USA committee
Susan Kenny, Peter Jennings, Jeri Laber, Anne Nelson,
Harvey J Kaye, Wendy Wolf, Rea Hederman, Jane Kramer,
Gara LaMarche, Faith Sale, Michael Scammell

Cover design by Andrea Purdie

Index on Censorship **(ISSN 0306-4220) is published
bimonthly by a non-profit-making company:
Writers & Scholars International Ltd,
Lancaster House,
33 Islington High Street, London N1 9LH
Tel: 0171-278 2313 Fax: 0171-278 1878
E-mail: indexoncenso@gn.apc.org
http://www.oneworld.org/index_oc/
http://www.coolbooks.com/
~outpost/pubs/index/indexoncenso.html**

Index on Censorship **is associated with Writers &
Scholars Educational Trust, registered charity
number 325003**

**Second class postage (US subscribers only) paid at
Irvington, New Jersey. Postmaster: send US address
changes to** *Index on Censorship* **c/o Virgin Mailing &
Distribution, 10 Camptown Road, Irvington, NJ 07111**

**Subscriptions 1995 (6 issues p.a.): £32 (overseas
£38 or US$48). Students £24/US$36**

© This selection Writers & Scholars International Ltd,
London 1995
© Contributors to this issue, except where otherwise
indicated

Printed by Martins, Berwick upon Tweed, UK
*Cover credits: (front) Peeping Tom (BFI STILLS/LUMIERE
PICTURES); (back and title page) Mae West in She Done
Him Wrong (BFI STILLS)*

Former Editors: Michael Scammell (1972-81); Hugh Lunghi (1981-83); George Theiner (1983-88); Sally Laird (1988-89); Andrew Graham-Yooll (1989-93)

Maverick muse

'No form of art goes beyond ordinary consciousness as film does,' wrote Ingmar Bergman in *The Magic Lantern*, 'straight to the emotions, deep into the twilight room of the soul.' Or, as Pauline Kael puts it, 'movies — which arouse special, private, hidden feelings,...can overwhelm us as no other art form, except, perhaps, opera, does.'

Film's power to move, to excite and to frighten is unique, which is perhaps why it has traditionally been feared by conservatives, and so often controlled or censored by totalitarian regimes, which have also made good use of it for propaganda purposes. Whether films can influence human behaviour or attitudes has been a subject of fierce debate since D W Griffith made *Birth of a Nation*, and it remains an open question. The debate is especially vigorous in the West, where a vogue for blood-soaked Hollywood gangster films is currently reviving calls by politicians in the USA and Britain for more censorship, particularly of violent videos. Although rapid advances in technology may well make screen censorship unworkable by the end of the century, the violence debate remains a very real issue, one that recurs in interviews and articles throughout this special number of *Index*. During 10 years as a film and video censor in the UK, I myself sometimes saw material which tested liberalism to the limits: images of sexual torture and mutilation; gang-rapes shot from the rapists' point of view; cruelty to animals; maimings or killings of the innocent by charismatic heroes (or heroines) for pleasure. Although the causality argument so freely used by the tabloid press remains unproven, to dismiss the genuine concerns of the public (especially parents) about the effects of sadistic images on the young, and even on certain kinds of adult, is surely premature. More research is needed, as well as much more openness on the part of the censors.

While debate in the western democracies focuses on sex and violence, censorship of film for political and/or religious reasons is still a grim reality in many parts of the developing world, where film-makers who dare to challenge the status quo risk imprisonment and death threats from

SALLY SAMPSON

fundamentalists. In China, the overseas success of films like *Farewell My Concubine* has not prevented censorship, and persecution of film-makers, at home. Elsewhere, in eastern Europe and South America, and parts of Africa, democracy has brought more freedom to film-makers — but at a price, as indigenous products compete for audiences with American imports like Arnold Schwarzenegger and Julia Roberts. Over on the other side of the Atlantic, the golden chains of the Hollywood studio system, with its obsession with market research and audience ratings, exert their own kind of censorship over creative film-making.

But cinema has always attracted outsiders, and original talent breaks through. We celebrate the emergence of exciting new women directors all over the world, and hear from John Waters, arch enemy of political correctness, about the future of the kind of cinema that constantly tests the limits of acceptability.

Along with procrastination, secrecy has always been a favourite weapon of film censors: lack of information stifles criticism and debate. In this tribute to cinema's centenary, *Index* puts the spotlight on a hidden subject. At the same time, it celebrates the courage of film-makers, past and present, who have dared to be subversive. ❏

Sally Sampson, guest editor for **Index** *on film censorship*

This special issue of Index on Censorship would not have been possible without the support of

Sir David Puttnam and Enigma Productions
The British Film Institute
The National Film Theatre, especially Mark Adams
UIP, especially Jane Montandon
Quentin Curtis
Nick James
Anne Logie
Susan Richards
Mark Rosin
Harriet Vidal-Hall
Henry Vivian-Neal
all the contributors

and most of all the patrons, committee and supporters of the premiere of Roman Polanski's *Death and the Maiden*, whose generosity provided the means to undertake this project

The Subversive Eye

To tie in with this issue of **INDEX**, the British Film Institute will be showing two banned films at the National Film Theatre in London.

The Days (Dong-Chun de Rizi)

Dir. Xiaoshuai Wang, China 1993
Starring Xiaodong Liu, Hong Yu.
Thursday, 23 November 1995
8:30pm NFT2

The Days is banned in China, and its director, like many other independent film makers, is blacklisted by the Chinese Film Bureau. '*The Days* is a delicately understated — but piercingly moving — account of the end of a relationship, which at the same time pin-points a mood of dread and incipient defeat that Wang clearly sees as endemic in China's present political climate.'

— Tony Rayns, *Sight and Sound*

Tony Rayns, film-maker, critic, lecturer and festival programmer with a special interest in the cinemas of East Asia, will be speaking at this showing.

Man of Marble (Czlowiek z Marmuru)

Dir. Andrzej Wajda, Poland 1977
Starring Krystyna Janda, Jerzy Radziwilowiz.
Friday, 24 November 1995
6:00 pm NFT1

Polish authorities limited the initial distribution and cut scenes relating to the 1970 police massacre of Gdansk shipworkers in Wajda's thrilling political drama about the power of the media to manipulate reality. In her first role, Krystyna Janda stars as a student documentary-maker trying to unearth the truth about the Stalinist years.

Tickets cost £4.50 and can be booked by telephone, in person at the door or in advance from the NFT Box Office, BFI on the South Bank, Waterloo, London SE1 8XT. Telephone: 0171 928 3232

INDEX

CONTENTS

Index and **WSET** depend on donations
to guarantee their independence and to fund research

The Trustees and Directors would like to thank
all those whose donations support *Index on Censorship* and
Writers and Scholars Educational Trust, including

The Arts Council of England
Charity Know How
The European Commission
The Financial Times
Ken Follett
Institusjonen Fritt Ord
The Norwegian Authors' Union
C A Rodewald Charitable Settlement

Stanley Kubrick's A Clockwork Orange, *1972 (see page 48)/Ronald Grant Archives*

The subversive eye

From its earliest days, cinema, with its unique power to capture the imagination and fire the spirit, has been in the censors' firing line. In the days of the Lumière brothers, as in our own, sex was the prime target. Today, violence has moved to the forefront of western debate. Elsewhere, film-makers may lose their livelihood — or their life — for daring to defy political or religious taboos. *Index* celebrates the power of the imagination that continues to challenge 100 years of film censorship

JOHN WATERS

BFI STILLS

Out on the edge

Did you make Pink Flamingos (1972) *and* Female Trouble *and all those early pictures with the specific intention of annoying the censors and the authorities?*

No, the reason for making those movies was to make me and my friends laugh. With *Pink Flamingos* I basically made a movie that would make fun of 'political correctness'. Obviously that phrase didn't exist then, but this was the early 1970s and there was still all that 1960s peace and love stuff around. So to make a movie for hippies that praised violence was very politically incorrect. What I was trying to do was to make all the liberals realise that *they* have limits even though they always think they don't. *I'm* a liberal, my audience is liberal, and what I'm always trying to do is to make humour about that grey line of how far you can go.

So you were trying to provoke a reaction of outrage?

I just felt that, whatever you thought about that movie, when you left you had to tell somebody. The ending was a word of mouth guarantee. It was impossible not tell somebody about it. Whatever you said: 'It was the worst movie'; 'It was the best movie'; 'I loved it'; 'It was disgusting...' Whatever. But no-one left that movie going 'Oh, it was OK.' It was *impossible* to have that reaction. In fact, in 1995, that film still outrages skin-heads! It still works!

Did you ever consider submitting it to the Motion Picture Association of America?

Are you kidding? Why waste US$200? But you know, I did always have a fantasy about submitting it to the Legion of Decency of the Catholic Church. Ha ha!

So which censor boards did you actually run into trouble with?

Well, because *Pink Flamingos* did play in regular movie theatres it did have to be licensed. We had a horrible censor board in Baltimore, one of the only states to have one, and it was headed by this woman who had a fourth grade education and used to say things on national television like: 'Don't tell me about sex, I was married to an Italian.' She was not an intellectual. But anyway, she watched *Pink Flamingos* and she only cut two scenes from the movie — she cut the artificial insemination, which *is* correctly the most repulsive scene in the movie, and she cut the blow job. She left in eating shit because there were just no laws against it. She couldn't find anything... I mean, who would *want* to eat shit? Which is exactly why I put it in. We got the best review in *New York* magazine which said it went 'beyond pornography', because who on earth wants to watch somebody eating shit? To this day, video stores don't know what section to put *Pink Flamingos* in; they can't put it in the X-rated section because who wants to jerk off and look at *Pink Flamingos*? So it's kind of funny that basically there were no laws on the book to deal with that, and the censors just didn't know what to do because they had never come across that problem. And that was sort of the point of the whole movie. To make a joke about what limits were. Anyway, after *Pink Flamingos* became a hit, *Multiple Maniacs* got to play in an above-ground theatre, whereas before it had just played in college theatres and so forth. So this particular censor had to see it, and when she got to the rosary job...well! She ended up saying: 'My eyes have been insulted for 90 minutes...but *it's not illegal!*' Because there weren't any laws about rosary jobs either. See, I was trying to come up with something ludicrous rather than the standard sex and violence which they have laws about.

What about the blow job in Pink Flamingos? *That comes close to porno.*

Actually, that's the one thing in the movie that does look kind of weird today. Remember that back in 1972 that blow job scene was really a joke about porno chic. *Deep Throat* had just come out, and for the first time hard-core pornography was available in above-ground theatres, and couples were going to see it. That was a huge thing at the time. Now no one pays attention, but back then *Variety* was reviewing porno, and it was the height of porno chic. And that's what that scene was: I was trying to do a joke about porno chic.

Deep Throat *was charged with obscenity in New York — what about* Pink Flamingos?

Yeah, *Pink Flamingos* was found obscene several times in America. It was found obscene *recently* in Orlando. When it came out in Hicksville, New York, which is on Long Island, we discovered that it was cheaper to plead guilty and just pay the US$5,000 fine. Because the film *is* obscene, but in a joyous way, which is very hard to prove legally. And when you show those films in a courtroom at 10am to a jury who have never met...believe me it's really frightening. They see it completely out of context. When audiences go to see that movie, they know what they're getting — they go to laugh, they go to be outraged. But with the jury, they don't know whether they're getting a burglary case or what, and then they suddenly get *Pink Flamingos*. And it looks *really* weird in a courtroom. It makes me shudder.

So what happened?

Oh, in the end Bob Shaye (head of New Line pictures) and myself had to pay a US$5,000 fine, and sign this paper that said if they ever showed it in Long Island we would go to prison. And at that time the Museum of Modern Art had just bought a copy for their permanent collection. They weren't impressed.

The one scene in the movie that I think shouldn't be there is the chicken sequence, not because it's obscene, but because it involves actual cruelty to animals. And I know that when I saw the movie play uncut in Britain, about half the audience walked out during that scene.

Well I know the chicken scene *does* offend people but I never get why, because (and I've said this before) we *ate* the chicken. We got it at a place that said 'Freshly Killed Chicken', so that's what you did every day —

you went in, got a chicken, killed it, ate it. With that chicken, we killed it, it got fucked, it went in the movie, and then we ate it. We made its life better than the other chickens that were there. Now, if we hadn't have eaten it, I guess from an animal rights viewpoint you could have complained. But since the cast actually ate the chicken that night — we barbecued it because we never had any food on the set — I think it is not morally wrong from any viewpoint. It was of course a joke on 'what are the taboos?' Basically I put this ludicrous thing in because no-one does it. It's a joke on sexual perversion, about the fact that all sex looks ridiculous when you think about it. I thought the real weirdness of that scene was about voyeuristically watching the chicken get fucked. That to me is sicker than fucking a chicken.

But doesn't that explain why so many people walk out during it? They clearly felt the same way?

Oh I guess, but for me I always thought it was hippies and liberals going (bleating voice) 'Oh, an animal was killed!' And I bet they had a chicken sandwich right before they went in there. That sort of hypocrisy is what always amazed me. And that is the kind of liberalism that always says anything is OK until it's in there in your own life. Look, I'm a liberal, and I know people who don't eat meat who are junkies. Now, I have a little trouble with that! Same way, I would argue that if people say 'How could you kill a chicken in a movie?' — well, if we *ate* it, and *they* ate chicken themselves in real life, then that to me is ridiculous and I don't understand it. But you know, it was 25 years ago, and I'm sure I wasn't thinking that when I wrote it. But I *was* thinking about taboos and what taboos are. For example, I teach in prison, and I showed *Pink Flamingos* once to a class that was all murderers. When it got to the scene where Divine eats shit, for some reason every black person ran out of the classroom and didn't come back, while the whites stayed. Now why I do not know. So this was a movie that divided murderers along racial lines!

What do you think is the role of the censors in dealing with movies that set out to explore the boundaries of taboos?

I'm against censorship completely, the main reason being that if you want to help a movie then try to censor it. The censors were always my best press agents. As soon as they tried to stop a movie, we would sell out.

Anytime it was in the paper that we'd got banned or busted, people would want to see the movie. It's common knowledge in showbusiness. If you really want to censor something, the best thing to do is just never mention it. So I'm against all censorship.

Does that extend to everything, to every kind of film-making?

Well, let me see. Am I against the censorship of real snuff movies? Well, I don't really believe there are any. But I remember that during the period when everyone was making a fuss about them I had all these people like legitimate mainstream journalists ringing me up and going (*sotto voce*): 'John, you *have* to get me a snuff movie.' And I'd go: 'Jesus! What are you calling *me* for! I don't know about *that*!' I don't like real violence. Fans send me all the time video-tapes of like when that newscaster killed himself on television. I *hate* that stuff, I *never* look at it. I censor myself. I just have no interest in it and I never play those tapes. But fake violence? I have no problem with it at all. My films were jokes on exploitation films. They were exploitation films for art theatres. That's very different. *Pink Flamingos* does not work in a downtown theatre that would play a straight exploitation movie. It doesn't work because it has irony in it, and real audiences of real exploitation movies do not like irony. They're not interested in it.

How do you feel about the fact that there are cut versions of your early movies available in Britain, for example? Because it seems far more ludicrous to me to issue a cut copy of Pink Flamingos *than to ban it in its entirety.*

Yeah, to me too. It's like going to see *And God Created Woman* with no nudity. What's the point? It's like going to see *Pulp Fiction* with no violence. It's taking the shockability out when that was the whole *point* of the movie. But censors just assume that people are stupid, that they can't make up their own minds to turn something off, or walk out of the movie theatre.

Have you ever seen anything that you think shouldn't be allowed to be shown?

Yeah, most movies I've seen! *Forrest Gump* in particular. God, when he started running across the country, I just felt like stabbing to death the people around me. I *hated* that movie, and I wanted to ruin it for others that were sitting around me...because I could feel their love. But if you mean from a moral point of view... Well, there's a movie called *Clean Shaven*, which I thought was impeccable, which had parts in it that were torturous, but I'm certainly glad I saw it. I love to go to the movies and be tortured, and be uptight. I think parts of *Natural Born Killers* made me a little uptight because it's the first time they made killing look sexy, and I think that's a very scary thought in America. But I'm all for someone doing that in a movie. So no, never have I gone to see something and thought: 'This should be censored.'

Divine, *star of* Pink Flamingos, *1972*

You know that Natural Born Killers *was actually banned in the UK for a few months while everybody agonised over whether it would turn audiences into serial killers?*

I heard about that. Ridiculous. But you know the scary thing for me is that your censors are smarter than ours. We're used to dumb censors, but smart ones are scary.

How are British censors 'smart', exactly?

Well, for a start they don't say things like: 'Don't talk to me about sex. I was married to an Italian for two years.' They put things in a 'fair' way, or so it sounds like they're fair. Also they're fairly intellectual and learned. In America the censors are morons and they're proud of it. And that makes them easy to deal with.

What are the other differences between Europe and the USA?

One thing I've noticed is that in Europe, you have a much harder time with violence and humour in movies. And I think the reason is that you don't have as much violence, whereas here [in the USA] we're so used to it every day. And I think it's because we hate it so much that we make fun of it. But you don't have to worry about walking down the street everyday and possibly being caught in a shoot out. But we *do* worry about that, so we make fun of it. And I think that humour is hard to translate.

But we do have slapstick comedy and violent humour. We can still understand why a movie like Sam Raimi's The Quick and the Dead *is funny.*

Yeah, but listen — when I was on the jury at Cannes, many people were outraged by that movie. I had jury members saying: 'How can someone from your country, which has so much trouble with guns, make this movie?' And that shocked me. But I told them the same thing — that we're so used to violence that we make fun out of it. But they were outraged. They thought it was serious, like they're going to show this movie and every black kid is going to go out and buy another gun. And I think that's just a cultural difference.

Do you have a message for censors around the world?

Sure: you're the best press agents for anybody that makes movies that you don't want people to see. Please keep talking about me. I wish I could *hire* pickets. I wish I could *hire* religious fanatics to stand outside my movies. Because it only buys me another month's rent. Those people help. When I had to fight those censors, it made my career more popular. But who actually sticks up for censors? I've never met anyone who does. Here's what I think all those people are really saying. That if they had a child that watches a horror movie and that supposedly 'makes them kill somebody', it's actually that the parents didn't do something right before they saw that movie. Not the movie. Don't blame the movie, blame yourself if you didn't raise your kids to know what's a healthy way to be scared. I can't see it from any direction. I even fight it the other way. I think that if children of eight years old go into a library, they should be able to get any book they want. If they're smart enough to have heard of *Naked Lunch* when they're eight years old, they're old enough to read it.

Is there any element of sweet revenge in being the kind of respected film-maker who gets to sit on the jury at the Cannes film festival, when once you were considered to be the maestro of filth?

No, because I never felt bitter. In fact, the press and other film-makers always seemed very fair to me from the very beginning. My films did polarise people, but there was a war going on culturally at the time, which is not going on now unfortunately. The thing is that when there is a cultural war, some of the best art and best movies and best music comes out because there's so much to fight. Film-makers that I've met over the years have always been very supportive because, hey, it's not like we were in competition! Also, I think most directors respect other directors as long as they have a specific vision that takes you into their own world, even if you don't want to go there. So I never felt that other directors didn't like me, and if you want to know the truth, the critics that hated me were the *right* critics to be hated by. We used Rex Reed's name on our publicity, for instance, and even to this day he has a personal vendetta against my films. We wait for the reviews like we would wait for Santa at Christmas, and then we just howl. When *Serial Mom* came out he said: 'How sad for Kathleen Turner that she should have to work with John Waters.' And he said *Hairspray* was disgusting. *Hairspray*! But the most famous one was his review of *Female Trouble*, which we stuck all over the poster, and indeed I still have it hanging on the wall in the office in front of me. He said: 'Where do these people come from? Where do they go when the sun goes down? Isn't there a law or something?' That helped more than any good review. Now, times are very different, but in the beginning, we didn't use positive reviews, we used negative reviews like that, or like that 'beyond pornography' quote. We used reviews that were worthy, reviews from 'straight film critics', who were just speechless. They really helped.

You say that things have changed since that period — that there is no longer a 'cultural war' going on. Do you think that there is anything around at the moment that's challenging?

Well, *Pulp Fiction* did over US$100 million, and I just read that in America it's the biggest order of video cassettes ever. So, come on, I think that's a cutting edge movie and that gives hope to young film-makers everywhere. Sure you have *Casper the Friendly Ghost* but then there's *Natural Born Killers*, which had stuff in it which I think pushed it to the edge.

I think Serial Mom *is a really edgy film.*

Oh, so do I, and believe me, I had so much trouble within the studio system trying to get that movie on the screen the way I wanted it. You don't know how hard it is to get anything past Hollywood. It's all to do with marketing tests. You know, they wanted me to have her convicted in the end, every horrible thing you could imagine.

Is there anyone around at the moment who, in your opinion, is doing what you were attempting to do in the early 1970s?

I wouldn't say there was anyone doing what I was doing, but there are certainly young film-makers doing incredibly edgy things that I respect very much. The movie I mentioned before, *Clean Shaven*, was extraordinary; Todd Haynes' *Safe* I thought was agony to watch too and total brilliance; I like Gus Van Sant's new movie *To Die For* very much, and I very much like a French movie called *I Can't Sleep* about two gay serial killers who kill old ladies. I just watched this English movie last night called *The Young Poisoner's Handbook*. I loved that movie, I thought it was one of the best first films I've seen in a really long time. And that is very much my kind of humour. The whole point is that when you're laughing at the mother being slowly poisoned to death, it also makes you squirm, and makes you feel guilty. I'm a big fan of that movie.

What about Cecil B Demented? *What can we expect?*

The script is due on 15 October and I'm working on it every minute, and I'm really very superstitious about talking about a movie at this stage — in fact, I don't know if they're even going to *let* me make it yet, because it's a development deal and the script is very edgy. It's about a young lunatic film-maker who kidnaps an A-list Hollywood movie star and forces her to be in an underground movie. He's a teen terrorist against the movie business.

OK, let me ask you a hypothetical question: what if somebody came up with US$25 million and said: 'Right John we want to remake Pink Flamingos *but with a big budget, good looking camerawork and good looking stars, but they'll still do all the same things...*

What, like Meg Ryan eating dog shit?

Exactly. If you made that movie, do you think it would still run into the same censorship trouble that the original Pink Flamingos *got into?*

Umm. No...maybe not, but...it depends. Do you mean it would still be as graphic?

Absolutely, but just glossily produced.

Well, I think it *would* still have trouble, but not as much. Because the very primitive (by which I mean 'bad') camerawork made people think that movie was like a documentary, and that really added to the scary part. I think the graininess and the cheapness of it all really gave it a further edge. Because if you made it slick, it would be...but then actually I don't know, because that would be a *different* kind of slickness. If you did a high budget version, where the trailer was fabulous but you still *really* had them eating dog shit and all that kind of stuff; I think it would still get you in a lot of trouble. What I would do is to make the sequel, which I wrote and which I got published but no-one would ever let me do it. At the end of that they fly away on a turd. So that's the one that I would do. ❏

Interview by Mark Kermode

PHILIP FRENCH

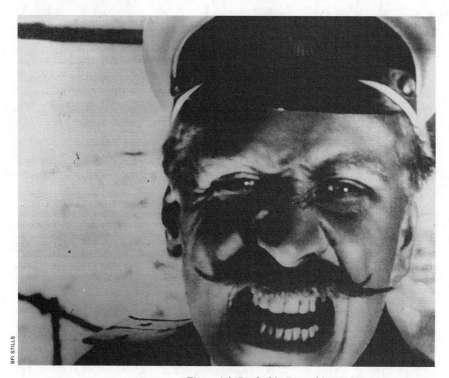

BFI STILLS

Eisenstein's Battleship Potemkin, *1925: propaganda coup*

No end in sight

When the noted UK film critic and scourge of the censors, Alexander Walker, heard that James Ferman, director of the British Board of Film Classification (as the British Board of Film Censors was re-named in 1985), was a member of the committee appointed to celebrate the centenary of cinema, he wrote a letter of protest to the committee's chairman. The reply he received referred to Ferman's probity, his devotion to the cinema and the obvious discourtesy that would be involved in seeking his resignation. A more robust response would have been to say that since its earliest days the movie industry has been in an unholy (though some would say a holy) alliance with the censors, that censorship had shaped the course of movie history and played a part in determining the language of popular cinema. It would thus be as unrealistic and disingenuous to refuse the censor a seat at the centennial feast as it would have been, 40 years ago, to deny the public hangman an invitation to a celebration of British penology.

Even before the first films were projected for a paying audience by the Lumière brothers in December 1895, the police had been intervening in Europe and North America to prevent peep-show machines from showing such innocently erotic items as *Dorolita's Passion Dance*, which was withdrawn in 1894 from the Kinetoscope Arcade on Atlantic City's Boardwalk. Whether there really was a sequence of flicker-cards or a few dozen feet of film called *What The Butler Saw* is, I believe, uncertain. But the title has entered the language and for good reason. It suggests three things — voyeurism, class and dangerously illicit activities observed and revealed to an outsider.

In 1896, one year after the Lumière show in Paris, 50 feet of film recording a gentle kiss between May Irwin and John C Rice, both middle-aged, from the Broadway play *The Widow Jones*, had US newspapers calling for it to be banned. The following year the moral opprobrium focused on screen violence as exemplified in a string of films bringing championship boxing matches to the general public. Terry Ramsaye, who lived through the period, wrote in the first comprehensive history of American cinema, *A Million and One Nights* (1926):

One marked effect of the Corbett-Fitzsimmons picture as the outstanding screen production of its day was to bring the odium of pugilism upon the screen all across Puritan America. Until that picture appeared the social status of the screen had been uncertain. It now became definitely lowbrow, an entertainment for the great unwashed commonalty. This likewise made it a mark for uplifters, moralists, reformers and legislators in a degree which would never have obtained if the screen had by specialisation reached higher social strata.

Shortly after the turn of the century, a Chicago judge claimed that the cinema was among the chief influences — bad, of course — on the juvenile offenders who appeared before him. His sentiments were echoed over 90 years later when the English judge in the James Bulger murder trial suggested that the juvenile killers had been influenced by the American horror movie *Child's Play 3*, though the local police could find no evidence that the children had seen it.

What was it that the benign American inventor, Thomas Edison, and his French friends, the photographic manufacturers Louis and Auguste Lumière, had unleashed upon the world, and that had so rapidly led to a demand for its control? The cinema developed during a period of unprecedented social change, and broadly speaking there were seven aspects that made it seem a threatening phenomenon (to which 30 years later was added that of rebarbative language and disturbing sound).

First, there was the very size of the image and the immediacy, the intimacy of the experience. Second, film opened up life socially, geographically, in time and space, transporting audiences to places unknown, hitherto forbidden, invented. Third, the violence and eroticism were palpable, yet they left the audience unscathed. Fourth, the cinema offered an invitation to fantasise, to dream, to revolt, and it is hardly surprising that the Futurists and the Surrealists were among the first to recognise its power. Fifth, the movies rapidly became the most popular leisure activity of the burgeoning urban working classes, feared by the bourgeoisie as a potential source of revolution and by intellectual devotees of eugenics as a threat to the future of Western Civilisation. Sixth, movie-going was a public activity that took place in the dark, offering terrible temptations to innocent boys and girls. Seventh, there were health and safety fears, some real, some imaginary: fear of fire hazards from unsafe buildings and highly inflammable nitrate film; fear that the flickering images might damage eyesight or induce epilepsy; fear that these hot, fetid auditoriums could spread contagious diseases.

Some early opponents of cinema wanted to crush the new medium in the bud. In 1986, Herbert Stone, the eloquent editor of the Chicago literary magazine, *The Chap Book*, wrote: 'I want to smash the Vitascope. The name of the thing is itself a horror. Its manifestations are worse.' Of the notorious Edison clip, universally known as *The Kiss*, Stone fumed:

When only life size it was pronounced beastly. But that was nothing to the present sight. Magnified to Gargantuan proportions and repeated three times over it is absolutely disgusting. All delicacy or remnant of charm seems gone from Miss Irwin, and the performance comes near to being indecent in its emphasised vulgarity. Such things call for police interference.

Wherever films were made or shown, censorship boards sprang up. Around 1914, American producers united to oppose officially constituted bodies, and the federal government refused to establish film censorship at a national level, though this was precisely what happened in virtually every other country. But a major blow was administered in a crucial judgement by the US Supreme Court in 1915. Delivering the majority opinion following an appeal by the Mutual Film Corporation against censorship boards in Missouri and Ohio, Justice McKenna stated:

It cannot be put out of view that the exhibition of moving pictures is a business pure and simple, originated and conducted for profit, like other spectacles, not to be regarded, nor intended to be regarded by the Ohio constitution, we think, as part of the press of the country or as organs of public opinion. They are mere representations of events, of ideas and sentiments published and known, vivid, useful and entertaining no doubt, but as we have said, capable of evil, having power for it, the greater because of their attractiveness and manner of exhibition.

This decision, denying the cinema the constitutional protection enjoyed by other media, was eventually reversed in 1952. But it set the tone for the way the movies were to be perceived for decades, at least in the Anglo-Saxon world, and continues to do so into the 1990s.

Meanwhile, in the UK, censorship came in through the back door. The 1909 Cinematograph Act was introduced to license cinemas for safety purposes and was extended by the courts to cover the movies shown in them. This led to the creation in 1912 of the British Board of Film Censors, initiated by the Home Office but run as a self-regulating body by the film industry, to license movies for public exhibition. Its second president, the ubiquitous T P O'Connor, Conservative MP, author and newspaper editor, served from 1916 until his death in 1929. During his reign, he made the film industry the acquiescent creature of the political establishment, a position from which it has yet to emerge.

Shortly after his appointment, O'Connor told a Cinema Committee of Inquiry that 'there are 43 rules and they cover pretty well all the grounds you can think of.' T P's rules, all of them prohibitions, prevented the production or exhibition of pictures involving 'unnecessary exhibition of underclothing', 'relations of Capital and Labour', 'realistic horrors of warfare', 'executions' and 'subjects dealing with India in which British officers are seen in an odious light'. We must remember that Britain was at war when O'Connor devised this list, but most of the rules remained in force for the next 40-50 years. Alfred Hitchcock turned away from political film-making forever when his plans to make a picture about the 1926 General Strike were rejected by the BBFC.

> The simple fact is that at every societal level we have been inculcated with the idea that censorship is necessary — to preserve society, to protect people from each other, to save ourselves from our baser instincts

It was some time before the US industry produced anything as detailed as T P's 43 Rules. But when it came, the Production Code was the most elaborate ever drawn up, and sought to make American movies acceptable and inoffensive to juvenile audiences at home and throughout the world. After World War I, during which US cinema began to establish the worldwide ascendancy that today seems unassailable, the Hollywood studios were coming under attack. Their films and the behaviour of their stars were agents of a changing post-war morality that small-town America found threatening. Anti-Semitism was part of this paranoia, directed towards a new industry largely created and owned by Jewish immigrants fleeing pogroms in Europe. In 1920, newspapers across the country carried an item with a Washington DC dateline that began: 'The lobby of the International Reform Bureau, Dr Wilbur Crafts presiding, voted tonight to rescue the motion pictures from the hands of the Devil and 500 un-Christian Jews.'

The response of the Hollywood moguls was to invite Will H Hays, a middle-western Presbyterian elder and postmaster-general in Republican

President Warren Harding's cabinet, to become president of the newly-constituted Motion Picture Producers of America Inc. The year was 1921, his job to put the industry in order to preserve its leaders' fortunes. He served them well for 43 years, and the present, only the fourth, person to hold this post is another recruit from Washington, President Lyndon Johnson's right-hand man, Jack Valenti, who became MPPA president in 1966.

Hays believed in the 'Ten Commandments, self-discipline, faith in time of trouble, worship, the Bible and the Golden Rule', and at one of his first Hollywood press conferences he declared:

> This industry must have towards that sacred thing, the mind of a child, towards that clean, virgin thing, that unmarked slate, the same responsibility, the same care about the impressions made upon it, that the best clergyman or the most inspired teacher would have.

He first introduced a system by which the studios were to submit to the Hays Office the books, scripts and stories they were considering for filming. Subsequently he sent out an informal list of what he called 'Don'ts and Be Carefuls'. The coming of sound with its possibilities for new verbal offence, along with the influx of irreverent new writers, many of them tough ex-journalists from big city newspapers, led to the adoption in 1930 of a Production Code drawn up by two midwestern Catholics, one a Jesuit professor of drama, the other a publisher of trade magazines. This Hays Office Code, made mandatory in 1934, began with three general principles — 'no picture shall be produced that will lower moral standards'; 'correct standards of life, subject only to the requirements of drama and entertainment, shall be presented'; 'law, natural or human, shall not be ridiculed, nor shall sympathy be created for its violation.' This was followed by eight double-column pages of detailed applications, ranging from the demand that 'no film may throw ridicule on any religious faith' to various proscribed words, including 'Fairy (in a vulgar sense)'. The Code was designed to make every film suitable for audiences of any age, and remained in force until 1967 when it was replaced by a system of certificated categories. This change was influenced both by European systems of censorship, and also by European films which, with their greater freedom in the handling of sexual matters, were making serious inroads in the American market.

The Code helped shape the language of Hollywood movies and the cinema worldwide, as writers and directors argued and bargained with the Code's administrators, and invented stratagems to approach forbidden subjects and metaphors to express proscribed acts. Fireworks and crashing waves stood in for sex. Body language could suggest the taboo subject of homosexuality. A woman with shiny lipstick, or chewing gum, or smoking in the streets, was identified as a prostitute. And the public came to take with a pinch of salt the come-uppance that the Code insisted be visited on glamorous villains. Yet there were whole areas of life that were ignored and distorted.

The industry was only opposed to external censorship. It was the major studios themselves who, through their control of production, distribution and exhibition, decided who would make films and whose pictures would be distributed. When Hollywood bowed to the House Un-American Activities Committee (HUAC) and other McCarthyite witch-hunters in the post–World War II years, a group of blacklisted film-makers produced *Salt of the Earth* (1953), an independent film about a miners' strike in New Mexico. They were harassed while on location by local and federal authorities, the leading actress was deported to her native Mexico, and the completed film was denied exhibition in the USA until the 1960s when it became a cult work among student radicals.

While this supposedly voluntary censorship was imposed in the USA, the movie-makers in the newly created Soviet Union were similarly having their talents harnessed to the cause of ideology. During the 1920s, artists were permitted considerable leeway to innovate and Pudovkin, Eisenstein and Dziga Vertov created a cinema that was revolutionary both politically and aesthetically. But with the coming of sound and the replacement of the enlightened Anatoly Lunacharsky by the philistine Stalinist cultural commissar, Andrei Zhdanov, Soviet cinema became rigidly controlled by bureaucrats and the doctrine of socialist realism strenuously imposed on the nation's artists.

Come the 1930s, and the German cinema, formerly among the least circumscribed, was taken over by the Nazis, though relatively few feature films were vehicles for explicit political propaganda. The European dictators of both left and right — Lenin and Stalin, Hitler and Mussolini — were fascinated by the cinema and aware of its power. They therefore sought to exploit it in their own interests. Artists working under them,

Hitler and Leni Riefenstahl on set 1935: a triumph of wills

including French film-makers of the Occupation and Eastern European cineastes of the post-war decades, could subvert censorship and censure by resorting to allegory, making movies with mythical subjects or putting them in historical settings. Likewise in Hollywood in the 1950s, when the studios were reluctant to make political films or touch on matters of race, these issues were dealt with in the guise of westerns or science fiction.

As the first great mass medium, the cinema provided the politicians and guardians of morality with the paradigm for censorship in the twentieth century. And, paradoxically in an era that has seen the democratic urge become central to social progress, there has grown up a culture of censorship, an expectation and acceptance of it. The least censorship — of films, as well as of the other arts and media — is usually found in confidently democratic countries that have recently experienced authoritarian regimes of the left or the right: in Greece and Spain, for instance, or Hungary and the Czech Republic, there is virtually no censorship of movies. But in countries that have not been exposed to such draconian treatment at the hands of the state, movies are subjected to pre-censorship that goes far beyond the methods of certification used to protect children. In Britain, for instance, where the Lord Chamberlain's role in licensing plays was abolished in 1968 and prosecutions of literary works are a thing of the past, the BBFC extends its influence and introduces new criteria. It is true that the situation has become increasingly permissive (despite a lurching, three steps forward, two steps back method of advance). But fashionable feminist sensitivities, about possible offences against women, for example, now affect the censors' judgements, and the BBFC's statutory powers to license video cassettes for home use has led to films for domestic viewing being subjected to an elaborate set of rules based on prurient and class-based assumptions about the way people (ie, the proletariat) see and perceive films.

The simple fact is that at every societal level we have been inculcated with the idea that censorship is necessary — to preserve society, to protect people from each other, to save ourselves from our baser instincts. Revolution, personal violence and sex forever lurk to disturb the status quo. And censorship is most evident in the cinema because, unlike books, plays, exhibitions, TV programmes and the radio, every film we see, every video we buy, is prefaced on the screen or on the cassette box by a certificate stating that the work has been examined (the British certificates are signed jointly by the Queen's cousin and the American-born James Ferman) and judged fit for us to see. It isn't in the interest of the film companies to reveal what the censor has excised for cinematic exhibition or video release.

One might suppose that there was enough official supervision. Sadly, the press, both popular and elitist, tabloid and broadsheet, are among the first to demand tighter control of the movies. Especially when it claims some gruesome murder has been influenced by a recent film. This isn't confined to editorial writers and sensational columnists. All too often movie critics demand that works that have offended them be cut or banned. The late Dilys Powell, the liberal critic of the *Sunday Times* from 1939 to 1975, gave evidence for the defence when D H Lawrence's *Lady Chatterley's Lover* was prosecuted for obscenity in 1960. Yet she claimed in 1948 that the innocuous gangster movie, *No Orchids for Miss Blandish*, should have been given 'a new certificate of D for Disgusting'. In 1954 she supported the BBFC's total ban on the Marlon Brando biker movie,

The Wild One: 'I am bound to say I think the Board was absolutely right.'

Recently we've experienced a new form of censorship as several critics employed by British national daily newspapers have called upon the minister for national heritage to investigate the financing from public funds in Britain and Europe of movies they disapprove of, either on moral or aesthetic grounds (ie, too arty or too sleazy). The films at issue are Michael Winterbottom's harsh road movie, *Butterfly Kiss,* and Mario Brenta's contemplative Italian picture, *Barnabo of the Mountains.*

Looking back over a century of movie censorship, like Beaumarchais' Figaro, one laughs for fear that one might cry at the fatuity and foolishness of it all. For 100 years, audiences have been treated like untrustworthy children, artists as enemies of society. The BBFC refusing a certificate for over 30 years to Eisenstein's *Battleship Potemkin* in case it should ferment mutiny in the Royal Navy. The same board, at the height of World War II holding up the distribution of *Western Approaches*, a documentary tribute to the Merchant Navy, because some torpedoed sailors in mid-Atlantic use the word 'bloody'. The French censors banning Stanley Kubrick's *Paths of Glory* in 1958 because it casts aspersions on the conduct of French officers in World War I, and Madame De Gaulle, 10 years later, attempting to have a film version of Diderot's *La Réligieuse* banned because it presented the eighteenth century Catholic Church in an unfavourable light. The Prince of Wales using his opening speech at the Museum of the Moving Image not to celebrate the cinema but to call for the banning of horror films on cassette — the so-called 'video nasties' — to protect his vulnerable children, and getting applauded by the audience of newspapermen. The Soviet authorities, unable to make any sense of Andrei Tarkovsky's autobiographical film *Mirror*, banishing it to the cinema circuit that served military bases. The New Zealand censors approving the Joseph Strick version of James Joyce's *Ulysses* only for exhibition to single-sex audiences. John Huston getting the word 'gunsel', a rare word (possibly of Yiddish origin) for catamite used by Dashiell Hammett in *The Maltese Falcon*, past the Hays Office censor, who thought it was underworld slang for a gun-toting gangster, which indeed it became after the film was released. One could go on forever, as indeed film censorship threatens to do. ❑

Cracking the code

Baby Face, *starring Barbara Stanwyck as Lily Powers, met with censorship problems shortly after its release in July 1933. The Hays Office recommended that the picture be pulled from the theatres for its violations of the Production Code*

James C Wingate, director, Studio Relations Department, MPPA, to Darryl

Zanuck, chief executive, Production, Warner Bros Pictures

3 January 1933 We have read the script of *Baby Face* and have given it very careful consideration. In our opinion it contains elements which will make it satisfactory from the standpoint of the Code. However, it is hard to judge a story of this type from the script alone since it depends almost entirely upon how it is treated on the screen as to whether or not it will prove acceptable. We have no doubt that you will take every precaution to supply such moral values as may seem necessary to counterbalance a story which without them might seem to stress to too great a degree the element of sex.

[It] is exceedingly difficult to get by with the type of story which portrays a woman who, by means of her sex, rises to a position of prominence and luxury. Since this is the theme of your story and since it seems to us that the details have been, for the most part, handled with care and taste, the only remaining thing to do is to treat the story in filming it as to minimize the element of sex and show through Lily's characterization that her sort of luxury and financial success does not bring any lasting happiness. Further, it might be wise to so revise the ending as to indicate that in losing Trenholm she not only loses the one person whom she now loves but that her money also will be lost. ...if Lily is shown at the end to be no better off than she was when she left the steel town you may lessen the chances of drastic censorship action by thus strengthening the moral value of the story.

As to the treatment of the relationships existing between Lily and each of her different men we believe that insofar as possible you ought to avoid making the facts of each relationship too explicit. This can be done by never really showing through dialogue or action that the man in each case is really paying for the apartment and supplying Lily with money and clothes in return for her affection...

James C Wingate to Jack L Warner, president, Warner Bros Pictures

26 April 1933 We still feel that there will have to be some fundamental change in the theme of the picture, if it is to meet with the full requirements of the spirit and letter of the Code.

First you should strengthen very much the conversation of the cobbler and Lily to indicate that he is advising her to get out of her sordid surroundings into a big city where she will have opportunities for legitimate material and cultural advances and with a definite suggestion that she should be careful not to pay the price of advancement with immorality.

Secondly...it will be necessary to so construct the ending to indicate that Lily disregarded the cobbler's advice, and in the end show her stripped of wealth and social standing, and thus drive home the point that the philosophy now in the picture, namely 'use your body for material advancement', has been entirely defeated and discredited...

11 May 1933 ...we would suggest an attempt to use the cobbler in a few

added scenes as the spokesman of morality...[including] a scene showing the cobbler giving her a good scolding... In this scene he would tell her emphatically that she was entirely wrong, had been going not only against his advice but against all moral precepts, and that she would never find happiness unless she regenerated completely, mended her ways and made retribution of her ill-gotten gains.

★ ★ ★

In February 1933, Paramount released **She Done Him Wrong,** *adapted from the 1928 Broadway hit* **Diamond Lil,** *written by and starring Mae West. It proved the biggest money-spinner since* **Birth of a Nation** *(1915) and made Mae West an international star.*

Harry Warner, head of Warner Bros, to Will H Hays

9 October 1932 Please wire immediately whether I can believe my ears that Paramount has arranged to make *Diamond Lil* with Mae West. Recollect it was absolutely definite that *Diamond Lil* was not to be produced stop I am not sending this wire as a protest but I want to know how to run our business in the future.

'Mae West is the biggest conversation-provoker, free space grabber and all-around box-office bet in the country. She's as hot an issue as Hitler.'

Variety

Pictures: Barbara Stanwyck in Baby Face *(previous page and left); this page: Mae West and chorus line from* She Done Him Wrong/BFI Stills/UIP

ISMAIL MERCHANT

The maker of dreams

Ismail Merchant was only seven years old when his passionate affair with cinema began. From his first film, the boy was gripped by the magic of Indian movies.

'It was *Mela*, starring Nargis and Dilip Kumar,' he recalls. 'The stars were so handsome, the story so painfully beautiful...and when they sang the song,' he muses, quoting extensively from its most famous lyric, 'I cried.'

Other films followed, classics of Indian cinema and its stars. There was *Jugnu*, starring the singer-star Nur Jehan and many others, including the great Raj Kapoor movies, *Aag*, *Andaaz*, *Awaara* with their lavish sets. V Shantaram, with his magnificent mythologicals such as *Shakuntala*, was another favourite.

Whether these films were ironic and questioning 'socials', or fantasies of the past, engaged with the growing 'westernisation' of India or immersed in its rich and ancient heritage of music and story, Indian cinema was unashamedly glamorous and fabulous. Stories, songs, actors transported people into an enchanted, if remote, world.

Never content with watching his dreams from afar, Ismail was determined to realise them in his own life. His first chance came when his family became close to an aristocratic family with whom they stayed on pilgrimages to Ajmer, the tomb of a famous Muslim saint. 'I would hear the grown-ups speak about Jaddan Bai (Nargis' mother) and Wahidan Bai, another celebrated singer who was married to the Nawab's aunt.'

Years later Ismail met Wahidan's daughter Nimmi when she called on the Nawab in Bombay. Ismail was entranced. 'She had exquisite eyes: piercing, hazel and arched eyebrows like swords,' he reminisces, lapsing into the language of Urdu poetry. 'She must have been 18, maybe 19. She took me to the premiere of her film *Barsaat*. We went in her green Cadillac and people threw flowers. It was her first film and she was an instant hit.'

Hooked by now with the glamour and the stardust, 14-year-old Ismail took to haunting Nimmi's house in Marine Drive, the exclusive area where many stars lived. Soon they were firm friends. 'We would go to the Eros cinema and watch English and American movies

Nargis in Mother India, *1957: screen goddess*

together and Nimmi would tell me I should become a film star so that we could play opposite each other.'

But Ismail had other aspirations: he wanted to make films — to run the show. 'Cinema creates this magic in one's life,' says Ismail. 'If used constructively, it permeates religion, politics — every kind of communication. Its power is huge.'

And it was his conviction that the fantasy and the thrill were accessible to everyone, if only they reached out, that prompted him to court the stars and bring them into the lives of his fellow students. 'I was president of the Music Society at university and I regularly invited the top stars to be the guests of honour. We could sell many more tickets if the visiting celebrity was a film star.

'We are the
biggest producer
of films in the
world. About 850
per year...
A man who
spends his days
earning barely
enough to live —
what does he
have left to him
in the evening?
Film and sex...
Realist cinema
has not worked
here... People
don't want to
see poverty. If I
have nothing to
eat, I'm not
going to spend
three rupees to
go and see a film
where they talk
about people
who have
nothing to eat.'

*Ravi Gupta,
National Film
Development
Corporation
(India) (Quoted
in Le Monde)*

'I invited Nargis once. She said she would have to come direct from her shoot to be there for the starting time of 6.30. When she still hadn't come at 7.30, I went to her house, Chateau Marine. She came to the door, relaxed — not at all as if she was going anywhere. Someone had told her the event had been cancelled. I told her no, it was on and I was here to collect her. She got dressed immediately and we got to the show in her black and white Riley just as people were beginning to think she wasn't coming.

'Movie stars,' he adds, 'are one step down from gods and goddesses. I'd say they're higher in status than politicians. Politicians have to court them to attend their campaigns and rally votes. Look at M G Ramachandran in the south — he's hardly less powerful than a god. He began as a film star. It's a reliable route for an idealist who wants to change things for the better. Become a film star first.'

Indeed, Nargis, and her husband Sunil Dutt who co-starred with her in *Mother India*, both became prominent politicians as did numerous others including Dilip Kumar, one of the 'Big Three' male superstars of the 1940s and 1950s, and Vyjayanthimala, the dancing megastar of the 1950s and 1960s.

'People associate them with their roles — and everyone wants to follow someone else's charisma and superior identity. That's why even though the quality of Indian cinema isn't the same anymore, the worship continues.' ❏

Interview by Shahrukh Husain

Sex and violence

Scarface *1932: 'unacceptable' to the Hays Office*

JANE MILLS

Screening rape

There is a gap at the heart of mainstream portrayals of male sexual violence to women — a silence

Ambivalence is a particularly painful form of dis-ease for an ageing 1968-er. My anti-censorship credentials were once impeccable. As an officer of a national anti-censorship society, I believed the right to see violent, erotic Japanese movies was a basic human right akin to that of full employment. Pornography was a bit more complex: you could be for it (liberal humanist) or against it (humourless feminist), but mostly it was part of the argument for female sexual empowerment.

Something changed. In 1990 I made a BBC documentary, *Rape: That's Entertainment?*, to explore the cinematic representation of male sexual violence towards women in Hollywood movies. The research involved viewing over 250 movies in which women were tortured, punished and inevitably silenced.

Old habits die hard. I would wake up possessed by strong anti-censorship certainty. By teatime my liberalism was in tatters: knee-capping, frankly, seemed too good for those who skilfully, and often lovingly, produced all these degrading, demeaning and dehumanising expressions of gynephobic phallocentricity. Ambivalence had arrived, I had to quit.

When contemplating living in Australia it was exciting to imagine a country where, unlike the UK, I was free to hire a video of *Reservoir Dogs*, where freedom of information was enshrined in law and whose classification laws state 'adults should be able to read, hear and see what they want.'

Within two weeks of arriving I was protesting the banning of the Spanish film *In A Glass Cage* from the Sydney Gay and Lesbian Film Festival. The chief censor overturned federal government legal rubric previously thought to exempt film festivals from legislation. I felt the old anger at having to discuss censorship and free speech rather than the much more important issues raised by the film — rape, child sexual abuse and the renaissance of European fascism.

Australian adults face even more censorship laws: pay-TV viewers will be denied movies restricted to those over the age of 18; and the principle of free speech is about to be further qualified by 'the need to take account of community concerns about...the portrayal of persons in a demeaning manner'. Similar legislation has already been introduced in New Zealand where 'demeaning' is further emphasised with the words 'degrading' and 'dehumanising'.

This wording is open to diverse interpretation. Casuists will doubtless delight in argument about whether the Munchkins in *The Wizard of Oz* represent the degradation of short people. Anti-censors gloomily predict the banning of classics such as *King Kong* and Australia's very own milestone film, *Jedda*, both of which have utterly demeaning portrayals of black peoples. And whose liberalism would not be tested by a show trial of Aldrich's *The Killing of Sister George*, which is devoid of a single frame of female sexual empowerment? But none of these are likely to be denied (re)classification.

Nor are the myriad mainstream movies with graphic representations of rape that indubitably will be produced in the years to come, although some might be subjected to the odd snip. While I have never been persuaded of any causal connection between filmic representation and human behaviour, there is something about the way popular culture is so wedded to representations of rape that gives me a bad case of the ambivalences. I think it's because of the way the audience is invited, often successfully, to collude in a sense of it never really having happened.

This, of course, is a device that reinforces powerful cultural myths, based on men's fantasies about female sexuality that maintain no rape ever happens. As, for instance, in the notion of woman saying 'no' when she really means 'yes'. Or that she secretly desires rough sex. Or that her behaviour means she deserves it. Then there's the rapist as 'mad beast' myth — neatly placing the rapist outside the ambit of human law. Central to the myths and an analysis of the filmic representations lies a gap, an elision, a silencing. It is, of course, the female voice, the feminine perspective that is silenced, missing.

An elision also lies at the heart of the new Australian censorship legislation. The word 'rape' is not actually mentioned, but the close connections between the female experience of rape and the various denotations and connotations of the words 'demeaning', 'degrading' and 'dehumanising' make for interesting analysis. All three words can be seen as part of a male displacement strategy rendering mute the female voice with her own definition of rape.

'Demeaning' means 'to lower in status or reputation' — a notion endorsed by laws that 'protect' a woman from public disgrace by banning publication of her name. 'Degrading' connotes 'impairment with respect to some physical property', suggesting a woman's chastity represents her commercial value and that a woman herself is little more than male property (when 'rape' entered English in the early fifteenth century, it denoted the violent seizure of goods or property). Degrading also connotes 'decomposition', offering a reminder of the guilt many abused and raped women feel — when treated like shit you can feel you are shit. 'Dehumanise' conjures up two male rape films: Boorman's *Deliverance* and Tarantino's *Pulp Fiction* in which the male victims are made 'less-than-male'; they are feminised and thus dehumanised. I can no longer endorse an old liberalism that perpetuates a female silencing. But I cannot endorse censorship that prevents discovery of the real story either.

Why is all this so much more problematic than pornography? Perhaps because, unlike porn where all is explicit, at the heart of mainstream cinematic representations of male sexual violence towards women, there is this gap and silence. But this ellipsis, by its very nature, provides a space for the invisible to be made visible and the mute to be given voice.

The renowned screenwriter Jean-Claude Carrière recently protested self-censorship: 'Every artist has an obligation to murder his father and rape his mother.' Aside from Carrière's androcentricity (how does a woman rape her mother?), on the whole I agree with him. His words remind me we have to analyse the most ancient stories of western tradition to discover how female and male sexuality has been constructed around naturalised representations of rape that posit women as innately vulnerable and dumb.

I chose to hold on to my ambivalence because although cinematic representations of rape provide a trope that denies the embodied female experience, they also reveal an elision which makes it possible to discover that which has previously been hidden. From this perspective we can launch protest and change. ❏

KATHRYN BIGELOW

Bigelow and Fiennes on set of Strange Days, *1995*

Vicarious thrills

Kathryn Bigelow's second feature was reviewed by the trade magazine *Variety* as 'undoubtedly the most hard-edged, violent actioner ever directed by an American woman', but she must have long since smashed her own record. That film — *Near Dark*, a 'vampire western' — had cannibalism, child sex and blood. *Blue Steel*, in which Jamie Lee Curtis's novice cop is stalked by a psychotic killer, had gun fetishes, rape, wife-beating and blood. *Point Break* had bloody shoot-outs and Keanu

Reeves's face in uncomfortably close proximity to the whirring blades of a lawn-mower. 'When Rembrandt died, he gathered everyone around him and said, "Mehr Licht, mehr Licht" [more light, more light],' joked Ron Silver, the murderer in *Blue Steel*. 'When Kathryn dies, she'll be saying "Mehr Blut, mehr Blut" — "more blood, more blood".'

Four years after *Point Break*, Bigelow has finally completed a new film: *Strange Days*, a futuristic thriller set in Los Angeles at the turn of the millennium. The city is dark, decaying, crime ridden, wracked by racial tensions. And, skulking through the wreckage is the charming Lenny Nero (Ralph Fiennes), a former cop who has gone to seed and now peddles black-market 'SQUID clips', electronic memories that are recorded directly in people's brains and enable buyers to relive, in playback on a small headpiece, a slice of someone else's life. We see a good deal of these SQUIDs in the course of the movie, vividly presented through the dizzy subjective camerawork. Hence the film's long genesis, since it meant building a camera that could replicate the movement of the eye. 'You take for granted how effortless that movement is,' Bigelow says, 'but you can't duplicate it with a 40-pound Panaglide.'

Human nature being what it is, the vicarious thrills in keenest demand are sex, rape, burglary, murder and, above all, 'snuff' scenarios in which the original person dies. And Lenny has the sales pitch down pat to hook new users — the choice of term is deliberate — of the highly addictive clips. 'I'm the Santa Claus of the subconscious,' he likes to purr.

It's a confident and unusual film — and a bloody one. This time *Variety*'s verdict was 'a technical tour de force...conceptually daring and viscerally powerful.' But the reviewer also found the sensationalist content of the SQUID clips 'morally questionable', and predicted that 'more than a few women will have problems with these scenes.'

Bigelow vigorously defends her movie. 'There's a sort of hunger that we all seem to share: a need to see, to live a life vicariously, even if for only one or two hours,' she says. 'It's something I explored back in 1978 in a short film called *Set-Up*. It was about violence, scopophilia and why we desire this intensity. *Strange Days* is also about watching and its consequences. So there is a common thread between them. But in *Strange Days* I wanted, at the same time, to embed that idea shrewdly within the narrative, so that it's not a diatribe imposed upon it as perhaps I was doing in 1978.'

Bigelow began her career as a painter — an 'abstract expressionist' as

Strange Days: *'technical tour de force, conceptually daring, viscerally powerful'*

she describes it — immersed in the avant-garde New York scene of the early 1970s. She worked with Art and Language, a group of mainly British artists, embraced semiology and liked to cite Roland Barthes. Her name appeared on the masthead of the high-theory culture journal *Semiotexte* — in an issue devoted, characteristically, to polysexuality — and she said she thought she'd died and gone to heaven on seeing Rainer Werner Fassbinder's sombre gay psychodrama *In A Year With 13 Moons*.

'Working along those lines you become very analytical about what you're doing, about the commodification of culture. Ever since art stopped being at the service of church and state, it has been in constant search of meaning and identity. But at the same time I never lost the desire to communicate. Cinema is *the* art form of the twentieth century.'

From her first feature, *The Loveless*, a languid, gorgeously designed biker movie, Bigelow has been nudging more and more towards the commercial mainstream: her films now are less likely to play at the Museum of Modern Art, New York, than at a multiplex near you. Today she will name as her favourite directors not Fassbinder but Walter Hill, Oliver Stone, James Cameron, with all of whom she has been associated and, in the third case, briefly married. Cameron co-wrote the screenplay for *Strange Days*. But she still believes it possible to make 'captivating' crowd-pleasers while maintaining a critical distance.

'The challenge is to make the material very, very accessible, but with a conscience. In *Strange Days* the SQUID clips are filtered through the character of Lenny Nero. And he, I think, helps us with our own reactions; he directs us, so to speak. His reaction, for instance, to the killing of Iris [one of the women] is one of absolute shock, horror and revulsion. In other words he mediates it for us.' So, she adds, does Nero's best friend, played by Angela Bassett, when she witnesses with horror a black singer and political leader being slain by police in a Rodney King-type incident.

To support this claim Bigelow cites her film's first scene: a long, long, apparently unbroken, subjective point-of-view shot of a robbery seen through the eyes of one of the criminals. The camera races through a house and across a roof as the police give chase; and then, as the thief leaps to another building and doesn't quite make it, he, and we, plunge to death.

'When I was in the cutting room, friends would come over and I would show them that footage. They stared at this tiny little screen, with no sound. They would sit back at first but, as we progressed along the sequence, I noticed them sitting forward and finally, as the camera runs up the stairs, their legs would be moving. So even in that small, crude format they are caught, they are participants in the experience. Now, in that opening sequence you don't yet have a person to identify with. But I do believe the events are mediated through an emotional investment in the characters once you've been introduced to them.'

She argues strongly against the notion that we might be 'victims' of progress: that, as film and the other mass media, including virtual reality technology, become more sophisticated, the audience becomes more and more sucked into the viewing process. 'The history of anything has been based on attempting to push the envelope and as film-makers we tend to want to use all the tools available. That exploration is always valid because it can create new images and new ways of thinking.

'Obviously now, with computer-generated imagery, it's possible to do almost anything; your only limitation is your imagination. And it probably does promote a more visceral response in the audience. On the other hand, I also think that the viewer is *responding* to that response at the same time. It's a relationship that is constantly ratcheting up the stakes.'

Strange Days includes a graphic and extended rape scene (as did *Blue Steel*). Oliver Stone would certainly have been sent to the doghouse for showing such material, and I wondered whether Bigelow, as a woman, felt she was able to get away with more than a male director would. 'There's violence against women in our culture; there's truth to that existing in our lives. It's not like it's being made up.

'In *Strange Days* it's the dramatic event that propels the rest of the story forward, not unlike the shower scene in *Psycho*. I boarded it very carefully. I walked through it shot by shot with the actors. Everybody was part of the process; we all shared in its necessity. It is not there for any kind of titillation or exploitation, but as an awful fact of our existence. So it really depends on how it's handled. Whether that is influenced by gender, I don't know, although I'm sure it has something to do with it.

'And we also had another woman who's a nice contrast. If Iris were the only woman in the picture, I would say "you're giving me no options, no other potential reality." But since Angela Bassett, who is all-empowering, who is the moral centre of the film, who is completely self-possessed, is there, it gives you a spectrum of identities to explore.'

Political correctness is only one of the pressures on US film-makers; on their other flank are right-wingers like Bob Dole, Dan Quayle and Michael Medved who hold Hollywood responsible for a multitude of sins. 'They're using the movie industry in a political game. Rather than turning their attention to the cause of the social ills that are being represented in a film they fault the errand-boy,' Bigelow says. 'It does make life more difficult but the struggle for freedom of speech is so on-going and so important that it probably entrenches you all the more.' ❏

Interview by Sheila Johnston

IAN BURUMA

A case of overkill

MANGA

E ven in the interest of its own tradition, the Japanese animated film, *Urotsukidóji* or *Legend of the Overfiend*, is exceptionally violent. It lasts for 108 minutes, and there is hardly a scene that does not contain some form of mutilation, torture, cannibalism or mass destruction. Cities are blown up, bodies are exploded, young girls are raped. But oddly enough, few people actually get killed.

The violent mayhem in *Legend of the Overfiend* is like the violence in Greek myth: people and gods do not die; they are transformed. A human body impregnated by a divine monster becomes monstrous in turn. The brutality is almost abstract, divorced from reality, as is the story itself.

The film shows a war of three worlds that coexist on our planet: the worlds of demons, of man-beasts and humans. Once every 3,000 years the Overfiend is born to unite the worlds, and purge them of sin, by breaking the barriers between them. Humans become prey to the evil of demons; man-beasts transform humans into demons; demons fight man-beasts. Monstrous giants, sprouting wings, horns and all the other paraphernalia of monsterhood, try to slay one another, while the world

— or rather a cartoon version of Osaka — burns.

Given its provenance, one is tempted to see this kind of thing as something peculiarly Japanese. To be sure, the visions of the apocalypse, of entire cities being destroyed in seconds, might have a special resonance in a country that is not only prone to earthquakes, but was horribly bombed too. Tokyo was almost entirely demolished twice this century: by the earthquake of 1923, and in 1945 by B-29 bombers.

Yet the story plugs into universal fears and concerns. The violent and often sexually induced transformations are common to adolescent fantasies everywhere, as well as to myths shared by most cultures. And the brutal revenge of a wimpish high school boy, who is given demonic powers, on the hearties who used to bully him, is hardly unique to Japanese popular entertainment. It is the form, perhaps, rather than the content that has some traditionally Japanese aspects.

As I write, I have in front of me a reproduction of a Hokusai woodblock print. It shows a naked woman under the sea being penetrated in every orifice by an octopus. An almost identical scene appears in *Legend of the Overfiend*, where a schoolgirl is assaulted by a monster, whose tongue is transformed into tentacles that envelop the girl. Apparently, in the full version of the film, the tentacles do more than that, but the British censors have made sure we cannot see it.

To censor an animation movie, such as this, for its sexual content is absurd. The censors applied standards of morally correct conduct to a mythical world. It is as though one were to fault Theseus or St George for being cruel to animals. As has been true of so much erotic art in Japan, sex is depicted in a way that is so deliberately grotesque that it is divorced from daily life. Like the violence in the film, it is pure fantasy.

There is, certainly, something disturbing about the movie, but this has nothing to do with the sex. Fantasies about purging the world of sin by staging an apocalypse led by divinely inspired figures, are uncomfortably close to the visions of violent religious cults, such as the Aum Shinrikyo, whose followers were willing to commit mass murder for their leader, Asahata Shoko. It should come as no surprise that the Aum members were avid fans of violent animation films. This should not, in itself, be a reason for censorship either. But of all things to be worried about in movies such as this, sex would seem a bizarre, not to say grotesque, choice.

JULIAN PETLEY

Clockwork crimes

Chronicle of a *cause célèbre*

The British Board of Film Censorship may have cut or banned some
worthwhile films in its time, but *A Clockwork Orange* wasn't one of
them. Indeed, Stephen Murphy, the BBFC's secretary at the time of the
film's release called it 'one of the most brilliant pieces of cinema, not
simply of this year, but possibly of the decade,' while his predecessor,
John Trevelyan, said that it was 'perhaps the most brilliant piece of
cinematic art that I have seen'. After it (and he personally) had been
subjected to a sustained campaign of vilification in the press, it was the
film's director, Stanley Kubrick, who withdrew it from distribution in
Britain, acting as the censor.

A Clockwork Orange appeared in Britain in January 1972 in the wake
of a number of films — *Soldier Blue, The Devils, Witchfinder General, The
Wild Bunch, Performance, Straw Dogs* — that had thoroughly shaken the
guardians of official morality and, as ever, the pundits of Fleet Street. The
critics tended to take a more tolerant, and certainly better informed, line.
Straw Dogs, however, seems to have proved the last straw for most of
them. They not only savaged it in their columns but 13 leading critics of
the day took the unprecedented step of writing a letter to *The Times* in
which they claimed: 'In our view the use to which this film employs its
scenes of double rape and multiple killings by a variety of hideous
methods is dubious in its intention, excessive in its effect and likely to
contribute to the concern expressed from time to time by many critics
over films which exploit the very violence which they make a show of
condemning.' Although not an overt call for censorship, it could hardly
have helped an increasingly beleaguered BBFC and certainly contributed
to the growing climate of hysteria being whipped up by the moral

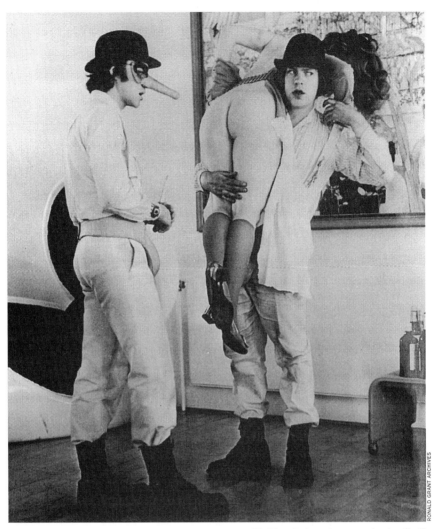

'Dubious in intention, excessive in effect'?

RONALD GRANT ARCHIVES

entrepreneurs and their allies in the press.

It is a tribute to Stephen Murphy and the BBFC that they passed *A Clockwork Orange*, and uncut, in such a febrile atmosphere. Unfortunately they reckoned without the notorious pusillanimity of the British distributors and exhibitors, many of whom, particularly Sir John Davis of Rank, were horrified at what they perceived as a disturbing new trend in cinema and were more than prepared to add their weight to calls for stricter censorship (while, of course, profiting from the offending items in the meantime). And so, to *The Times* letter from the critics was added the

On violence

Of course everybody is worried about screen violence, of course everybody stigmatises it. What nobody seems to point out is that screen violence opens up dark corners and exposes to public scrutiny a side of life that might otherwise remain hidden. War; torture by the military or the police; gangsterism; criminal behaviour by friendless young people without hope or money — these are blemishes on the body politic that society prefers to ignore. Occasionally, films can open people's eyes.

Do violent films incite violence? I don't believe a word of it. Since Aristotle's day, it is common knowledge that people go to public entertainments to purge their baser instincts, and that they return home calmer. They are liberated, not corrupted, by the screen depiction of criminal perversions. Although it is possible that maladjusted or disturbed people might get new ideas they had never thought of before from works of imagination, this is only an assumption.

In my films, the violence is urbane, civilised and restrained. For, to be convincing, fictional violence has to be less graphic than what you see on the television news. In my films I want violence to be placed in its proper moral context; I want it to be properly understood.

© *Claude Chabrol,* Et Pourtant Je Tourne... (*Editions Laffont-Fixot, 1976*)
Translated by Sally Sampson

even more extraordinary spectacle of the trade paper *CinemaTV Today* headlining its front page of 11 March 1972 'Murphy Must Go' — because he was too loath to cut and ban films!

According to Rive, then president of the Cinematograph Exhibitors' Association, Murphy was 'the wrong man for the job', and he added that as 'the film industry appoints the censor, so it is up to us to put our house in order by getting rid of him. He has got completely out of touch with public opinion.' So out of touch, in fact, that in the 1972 list of top 20 box office hits *The Devils* came fourth, *A Clockwork Orange* eleventh (quite remarkable considering that Kubrick, disturbed by the campaign against the film, persuaded the distributor to delay considerably the film's release outside London), and *Straw Dogs* fourteenth!

The reason for the distributors' and exhibitors' craven attitude was, of course, their fear of the spectre of local censorship — to ward off which the BBFC had been formed in the first place. Alerted by lurid and sensational stories in the press, certain local authorities had now begun to ban films that had been passed by the BBFC — *The Devils* in particular falling victim to council public health and licensing committees, fire brigade committees and all sorts of other committees utterly unfitted to sit in judgement on films — let alone films that had been distorted out of all recognition by malicious and ill-informed press reports.

Local council moral entrepreneurship was given an undoubted boost, and a spurious legitimacy, by the stories of 'copycat crime' that rapidly attached themselves to *A Clockwork Orange*. Indeed, this scenario was laid out even before any such alleged crimes actually took place. In an article in the *Evening News* on 27 January 1972 entitled 'Clockwork Oranges Are Ticking Bombs', the Labour MP Maurice Edelman prophesied that 'when *Clockwork Orange* is generally released it will lead to a clockwork cult which will magnify teenage violence.' And, sure enough, by May the papers were alleging that the film had indeed led to violent crimes being committed. However, and not entirely unexpectedly, the stories simply do not bear close scrutiny. For example, the *Mail* of 8 May 1973 stated that 'a "Clockwork Orange" gang was being sought last night after the murder of a 50-year-old firewood seller' in Newton-le-Willows. However, the only 'evidence' that the paper adduces to link the murder to the film is the fact that it took place 24 hours after the film finished its run at a local cinema, and teenagers had been buying clothes and make-up similar to that worn by the Droogs in the film.

Much more coverage was given to the case of Richard Palmer, who murdered a tramp in Bletchley. The *Mail* of 4 July headed its story 'Why "Clockwork Orange" Boy Murdered a Tramp', but then rather spoiled things by revealing that Palmer hadn't seen the film (as he was only 16 he wasn't entitled to do so anyway) but had simply read the book which, his mother is quoted as saying, had not affected him. The dubious *Clockwork Orange* comes in only because a consultant psychiatrist called by the defence opined that 'it seems to me the boy was acting a part which seemed very similar to the characterisations given by *A Clockwork Orange*: I believe the main theme of the book is this feeling of hostility from the younger to the older generation.' He is then echoed by the defence counsel who asks, somewhat rhetorically: 'What possible explanation can there be for this savagery other than this film?', although the answer, rather more prosaically, is actually 'robbery'. Once the notion of such crimes became firmly embedded in the news agenda it became increasingly tempting for defence counsel, especially when faced with a seemingly hopeless case, or a judge who appears to believe everything he reads in the papers, to push the *Clockwork Orange* button and hope for the best — or at least a lenient sentence on the grounds of mitigating circumstances.

As with so many British censorship *causes célèbres* it's hard not to read about the trials and tribulations of *A Clockwork Orange* without coming to the conclusion that the real villain of the piece is the British press with its uniquely awful combination of prurience and censoriousness. There's something particularly disturbing and outrageous about one section of the media calling for the censorship of another — particularly when, as the privacy debate over the past few years has shown, the press reacts to threats to its own considerable freedoms with howls of outrage and fury. It was only in Britain that *A Clockwork Orange* was subjected to a campaign of vilification in the press. It is only in Britain that Stanley Kubrick has decreed that the film may not be shown in cinemas. These two facts are not, presumably, unconnected. ❏

BERNARD WILLIAMS

Muted mutations

When the Report of the Committee on Obscenity and Film Censorship came out in 1979, the discussion of cinema was particularly criticised. The recommendations themselves — to maintain, with changes, the existing certification system — were not too controversial. The complaint was that, having taken a fairly cool tone about the alleged effects of violence and pornography in other media, we seemed to have been excitedly over-impressed by our experiences at the movies, and went on in strong and not very scientific terms about the power of film.

There was something in the complaint. In part, our tone was no doubt affected by the untiring efforts of James Ferman (still director of the BBFC) in showing us material that had given the Board problems. We spent more time receiving evidence about film than about any other subject and less time, perhaps, thinking about it.

Nevertheless, it still seems to me that we were right to acknowledge the special power of film to excite and disturb (though not necessarily to incite to violence). Some of our critics suggested that we had this idea because, being naive academics or other worthy people, we had not spent much time in the cinema. On the contrary, if we were too open to this idea, it was rather because, being of a certain age, some of us had spent only too much time in the cinema, and understood the unique experience of being submerged in the darkness, alone with others who were alone, dominated by the image.

Is that experience still the same? In particular, now that videos exist, is watching a film in the cinema the same as merely watching a film? Videos barely existed in 1979, and the Committee said nothing about them. There is now, of course, a certification system for videos, modelled on that for the cinema and run by the same agency. In a way, this speaks to the idea that the experience of film (of *The Silence of the Lambs,* for instance) is much the same for a given age group inside a cinema and out of it. But do we really think this?

Everyone knows that the system works, at best, only in a very haphazard way. Millions more youngsters and, indeed, children will have seen *The Silence of the Lambs* on video than could have seen it when those under 18 had to find a way of sneaking into a cinema. In some connections we think, as the Annan Committee thought about TV, that we should be more careful about what turns up in the home than in a cinema. But this is not how the system works. The videos are classified, but the labels have less effect in the home than in the cinema.

Perhaps we merely have a feeble system which we make out to be stronger than it is. But I suspect that there is more to be said: the actual outcome, to some degree, makes real sense. This is because film *is* film in the cinema, and its disturbing effects are above all effects in the cinema. A domestic video does not offer the showing of a film, but a by-product, a record or a trace. It can of course have disturbing effects, but typically they are muted and dissipated. Regulators can indeed do less about videos than they can about the cinema, but equally the videos can do less to us.

KEVIN MACDONALD

Poor Tom

'The only satisfactory way to dispose of Peeping Tom would be to shovel it up and flush it swiftly down the nearest sewer. Even then the stench would remain.'
Derek Hill, Tribune, 29 April 1960

'From its slumbering, mildly salacious beginning, to its appallingly sadomasochistic and depraved climax, it is wholly evil.'
Nina Hibbin, Daily Worker, 9 April 1960

'— neither the hopeless leper colonies of East Pakistan...nor the gutters of Calcutta — has left me with such a feeling of nausea and depression as I got this week while sitting through a new British film called Peeping Tom.'
Leonard Moseley, Daily Express, 8 April 1960

The vicious critical reception meted out to Michael Powell's *Peeping Tom* on its first release in April 1960, has entered into film folklore. Now that the film is widely regarded as a masterpiece, critics look back on their predecessors' philistine opinions and bask in a sense of critical — and moral — superiority.

Arguably, nothing has done *Peeping Tom*'s reputation more good than those original negative reviews. When re-released last year the film benefited enormously from the backlash: from toilet-flushing to masterpiece in 30 years. It made great copy. The most frequently repeated assertion had it that *Peeping Tom*'s despicable reviews effectively finished Powell's career, turning him into a pariah who could never work again in the British film industry.

In fact, Powell returned to directing the following year with *The Queen's Guards*, a uniformly poor film and a critical and box-office disaster. It was Powell's third flop in a row and, at a time when his anti-realist aesthetic was highly unfashionable and the British film industry in even worse financial straits than usual, it was enough to end any career.

It is tragic that one of Britain's greatest directors was prevented from making the films he so desperately wanted to make and was reduced to directing TV episodes and Australian B movies, but it isn't, directly at least, the fault of the British press and their reaction to *Peeping Tom*.

Today, as in 1960, film financiers don't care about reviews: what they care about is bums on seats. Then, as now, critical outrage was often good for business — witness the phenomenal success of Hitchcock's *Psycho*, which received reviews almost as appalling as *Peeping Tom*'s only a few months later.

The real harm caused by the reviews was indirect, and not necessarily attributable to the critics themselves. For example, on 25 May, the *Daily Mail* reported (disapprovingly) the actions of the 'watch committee' of Reading Town Council, which banned *Peeping Tom* from being shown in Reading without having seen it, purely on the basis of the national reviews. This despite the fact that the film had been passed but heavily cut for viewing by the British Board of Film Censors with an X certificate (suitable for over 16s).

A second effect of the bad reviews is harder to substantiate but more insidious. Alexander Walker — not a fan of the film then or now — related last year in the London *Evening Standard*, that Nat Cohen, owner of Anglo-Amalgamated, *Peeping Tom*'s financiers and distributors, voluntarily withdrew the film from circulation more rapidly than would normally have been the case because he was afraid its 'bad odour' would prevent him from being awarded a much-coveted knighthood. *Peeping Tom* was thus prevented from going into profit, and Powell's career doomed.

One can only conclude that the real villain in the case of *Peeping Tom* was not the press but the British Establishment. For all their narrow-minded and aggressive loathing of the film, as far as I am aware none of the critics called for tighter censorship or suggested a ban.

Instead of congratulating themselves on their open-mindedness and moral superiority in relation to *Peeping Tom*, modern critics would be as well to look at the state of the *Daily Mail* today, with its orchestrated smear campaign against Channel Four and cries for bans left, right and centre — and worry.

QUENTIN TARANTINO

Reservoir Dogs, *1992: 'small film…wild action'*

It's cool to be banned

*R*eservoir Dogs was designed as a really terrific small film, whereas *Pulp Fiction* is designed to be an epic in every shape and form: in size, in feel, in ambition, in intention, in look. *Dogs* is like a wild action painting, whereas *Pulp* is much more of a tapestry, more of a 'sit back and come watch the movie unfold.' If you were to leave during the first hour of *Pulp Fiction*, you can't even begin to say you've seen the movie. You really need to see the last scene before you can say, 'Yes, I've seen the movie.' That's a little unusual, because with most movies, once you've seen the first 10 minutes, you can say pretty much that you've seen the movie.

Some people who claim to have seen *Reservoir Dogs* just had a conversation with somebody about the torture scene. The annoying thing is that the torture scene in *Dogs* is my favourite scene; I think it's terrific (so did my mom). I can't think of a movie that came out during the last five years where one scene has been talked about as much as the torture scene in *Reservoir Dogs*. And the problem with that is that the movie has a lot more to offer than that one scene. But it's such a big mountain that people who could have totally handled the movie were scared of it. I was at the *Evening Standard* Awards back in 1992 when the film came out, and I met Emma Thompson.

The easiest way to kill the excitement and cult of something is to make it readily accessible

We started having a really nice conversation, chatting away, then she goes, 'I hate to say it, I'm scared of seeing your movie!' I go, 'Really? Oh well, OK.' And then she goes, 'But I saw *Goodfellas* and I loved it!' But *Goodfellas* is four times more violent than my movie! She said she saw *Henry...Portrait Of A Serial Killer*. I go, 'You can totally handle my movie if you can handle those! There's nothing to be scared of, baby!'

I actually kind of get a kick out of the fact that you can't get it on video [in the UK]*. It's because it's worked out fantastic for me! It's been playing for two-and-a-half months in a re-release. I didn't believe it when I was in Nottingham when they did the re-release. They all went, 'It's so cool, it's a big re-release, big deal!' I figured it would last about four weeks. I came back and got *Time Out*. 'OH MY GOD! IT'S STILL PLAYING!'

To be truthful, I could care less about the video thing. I think it's cool; I think that's terrific. If they were to cut a frame of the theatrical, I might be banging at the doors of Parliament. But as far as the video is concerned, the easiest way to kill the excitement and cult of something is to make it readily accessible. I always remember back in the days when I was a film-geek, hanging out with my friends, how we were always trying to see the sort of film that you couldn't see, like Jodorowski's *El Topo*: it was completely out of circulation, there was no way you could see it. And the Rolling Stones film, *Sympathy For The Devil*, there was no way you could see that, you couldn't find a print of it anywhere. One of us would get a copy, a horrible, screwed up one — the more screwed up it was the cooler it was — we'd sit around and watch this bad copy, (oh man, so cool, get this ripped, crappy old copy of *El Topo*, look at that, oh boy! you know!)

Spielberg talked about that with *ET*. That's one of the reasons he said he kept *ET* from selling to video for such a long time. Because, he said, 'I worked so hard on *Close Encounters of the Third Kind* and something just diminished all my hard work when I saw that you could have a video cassette of it just laying on your TV set, ready for you to play at any time. At least if you were going to look at a print of it, you'd have to carry a bunch of cases of heavy film, you'd have to exert some sort of effort in order to view it!'

I don't want my films to be disposable. I hope they'll last for hundreds of years. That's the thing that's great about film, that I can make one, and all the critics say, 'It sucks!', but if you've made a good film and nobody got it at the time it came out, history will be the ultimate test and you'll get recognised sometime, five years, 10 years, 25 years from now, and it will find its audience if it's good.

It's like pulp fiction: it was garbage fiction, you'd buy it for a dime, read it, and then you gave it to your mate — or threw it away. You read it on the bus to work, you put it in your back pocket and sat on it all day, and that was that. At the time it was completely disposable; and at the time it got no recognition whatsoever. But now all those authors are very well known; now you put it in your library! I don't like being presented with 'Here's this Art.' It's the same with exploitation films: they were presented that way when they came out, but some of them were absolutely fantastic, and they really affected me and my aesthetic.

I go over the moon when a film-maker I like has a smash hit; it gives me great faith in the industry. Looking at *Sweetie* and *An Angel At My Table*, would you ever have guessed that Jane Campion was going to do a movie that would be a monstrous smash all over the world? But she did! *The Piano* was a smash — as big as Jack Nicholson — in Europe! When an artist clips into the consciousness, doing their thing, that's the greatest thing in the world! ❑

© *Edited excerpts from Kaleidoscope courtesy of BBC Radio Four*
* Reservoir Dogs *was finally passed on video in June 1995 after two years' delay*

MARK KERMODE

Horror: on the edge of taste

Horror films present the censor with a problem: how to make 'acceptable' a genre that deals with the 'unspeakable'

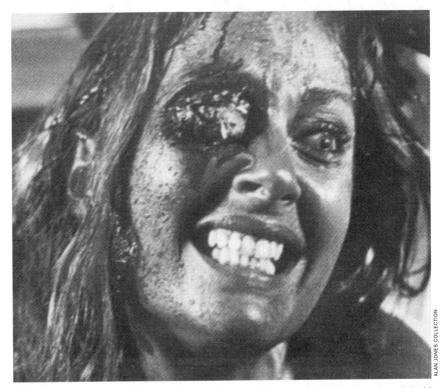

ALAN JONES COLLECTION

Zombie Flesh Eaters, 1979: tedium relieved by a 'moment of shock'

The Evil Dead, *1983: publicity shot*

'The difficulty with The Evil Dead *is that the name of the game is excess in the first place. To cut something that's meant to be over the top, so that it's no longer too far over the top, is very difficult...'*
British chief censor James Ferman, May 1990

Like its literary antecedents, horror cinema has always focused in upon the fluctuating boundaries of taboo. It is, by its very nature, a genre of film-making which relies upon transgression. It demands that the audience's sensibilities be affronted, that decency be damned (albeit temporarily), that rules be broken. Although sadly little mainstream horror cinema challenges its audience to reassess the nature of taboo (Stephen King argues that visions of monstrousness simply make us feel more comfortable with the norm), even the most narratively reactionary, moralistic horror movies feed upon the ecstatic shock of speaking the unspeakable, of showing the unwatchable.

To the censor, horror cinema presents an insurmountable problem; how to make acceptable a brand of film-making which, at its very best, strives to be thoroughly unacceptable? Their answer, to the eternal detriment of the genre, has been clumsily to neutralise and anaesthetise cutting-edge horror movies, blunting their very point and (more often than not) stripping them of whatever radical power they once possessed. For those few movies whose power remains undiminished by the piece-meal hatcheting of key scenes, outright bans are enforced as a last resort. Ironically, to the censor, the more inventive and effective a hard-core horror movie, the more likely it is to be butchered and banned. Only anodyne or unchallenging mainstream fodder can expect to be whisked through the censors' hands intact.

To highlight this problem, let us turn our attention toward the British Board of Film Classification (BBFC), a body that exemplifies the fundamental inability of censors to deal with horror cinema. A small and relatively conservative island, Britain has for many years been sheltered from the more excessive traits of European and American cinema by the BBFC, which classified and cut (or rejected outright) films submitted for public exhibition. Like the Motion Picture Association of America (MPAA), the BBFC has no legal standing in the cinema, but is purely an internal self-regulating 'advisory' body. Nevertheless, local councils with whom the power to permit or ban the exhibition of films resides, respect and enforce the BBFC's decisions, with few exceptions. As a result, films without BBFC certificates are effectively banned from exhibition in Britain.

Despite former chief censor John Trevelyan's 1973 declaration that cutting movies intended for adults was pointless, the BBFC have diligently hacked away at any material that could be considered contentious for years. When dealing with horror films, their penchant for cutting the visual pay-offs from which horror derives much of its visceral power and pleasure is extraordinary. Only in Britain could a horror fan be asked to tolerate the tedium of Lucio Fulci's *Zombie Flesh Eaters* without the reward of the movie's single moment of startling shock: the on-screen piercing of an eyeball, which stares in disbelief at an approaching wooden stiletto. The effect, to which British horror fans have long become accustomed, is not unlike listening to a comedian's routine from which the punch-lines have been studiously removed. One can only imagine how funny the act was intended to be.

More disturbingly, a number of taboo-breaking horror classics whose artistic integrity has proved unbreachable by the censors' scissors have simply been banned outright in the UK. In the mid-1970s Tobe

Hooper's *The Texas Chainsaw Massacre* and Wes Craven's *Last House on The Left* (both of which are now widely regarded as milestones in the development of horror cinema) were banned in their entirety after cuts failed to diminish their power. 'It's a very difficult film to cut,' said BBFC chief censor James Ferman of *The Texas Chainsaw Massacre*, which was submitted to the Board three times in various states of dismemberment, only to be airily dismissed each time. 'There's so little actual on-screen violence. However, there's lots of mental torture. It's almost impossible to change the nature of the film.' In other words the movie (which acclaimed director John Carpenter has correctly described as 'riding brilliantly along the very edge of taste') was simply too well-constructed to be rendered impotent by cuts. The result — an outright ban.

In the 1980s, the British censors' campaign against challenging horror movies was given an ironic boost by the rise of video. In its infancy, the video industry provided the UK with the only audio-visual entertainment which was not subject to some form of institutionalised regulation, other than notoriously vague obscenity laws. Spotting a loophole in the cinema censors' tight net, a few industrious entrepreneurs on both sides of the Atlantic took the opportunity to release on video movies that had previously been denied general theatrical exhibition. In the USA (and indeed much of Europe) this new medium would prove a saving grace for horror movies: despite the often stringent regulations of the MPAA, which still forces directors to cut or tone down their work for mainstream cinema release, distributors remain free to release unrated, uncut movies on videotape. Although certain chains like Blockbuster Video refuse to deal in such material, a relatively wide specialist audience can be reached through independent video outlets, mail order, and even record and book stores. Hence, unrated videotapes of horror classics such as *Blood Feast, Last House on The Left* or *The Texas Chainsaw Massacre* are generally available in the USA, as are uncut versions of such mainstream fare as Tony Scott's *True Romance* and Paul Verhoeven's *Basic Instinct*.

In Britain, however, the situation is quite the reverse. After an early anarchic heyday in which such international horror classics as *Driller Killer, Cannibal Holocaust* and *I Spit on Your Grave* became briefly available on UK video, tabloid newspapers mounted a campaign against the new 'threat', which they labelled 'video nasties'. In a wave of media-promoted

Rejected

[On 23 April 1994] a [South African] Committee of Publications found the video [*Braindead*] undesirable in terms of the Publications Act. The Committee motivated its decision as follows:

'This horror film (with elements of black comedy) has no merit whatsoever and is probably aimed at an adult likely viewership...

'The story revolves around Lionel, a young man who is very much dominated by his mother, who attempts to survive in horrific circumstances. Years ago some rats came ashore and raped the indigenous monkeys. A new breed — rat monkeys — appeared. It so happens that when these rat monkeys attack human beings, they start behaving in the same manner. When Lionel's mother is bitten, a series of gruesome incidents start to happen. People become monsters, attacking each other, eating each other, producing children who eat their way out of the womb. Those that die, stay in their graves for only a matter of time, come back as decomposed bodies and go on with their sickening way of life...

'The film is extremely scary, sickening, nauseating, disgusting, gruesome, filthy and, inter alia, degrading. It is actually quite impossible to find words to describe the bloody violence and cannibalism. Enough to say that there is not one redeeming factor. Even for a film in the horror genre this one goes just too far and totally exceeds the tolerance of the reasonable South African viewer, who would be offended by it within the meaning of Section 47(2) (a) of the Act.'

The Board subscribes in all material aspects to the findings of the Committee... The film, albeit not scary in the normal sense of the word, is nauseating and disgusting to the extent of becoming subversive... Excisions pose no feasible solution, as more than 50 per cent of the film would probably have to be removed...

On these premises the appeal is dismissed and the decision of the Committee confirmed.

D W Morkel, chairman of the Publications Appeal Board in the appeal of Nu Metro Video against a decision of a Committee of Publications that the video, Braindead, *is rejected in terms of Section 47(2)(a) of the Publications Act, 1974. 19 May 1994* hysteria, which would be bizarrely repeated 10 years later, horror videos were promptly blamed for everything from inattentiveness at school to muggings and rape, with headmasters, clergymen and politicians calling for drastic measures to protect the country from video dealers, who were labelled 'merchants of menace'.

Ironically, most video dealers were as eager as anybody for some form of regulation to be implemented since it was them, rather than video distributors, who were open to prosecution under the Obscene Publications Act (OPA) if their wares were judged objectionable. There were, at that time, no official guidelines as to which videos were unacceptable, and even films that had been passed for cinema release were not safe from prosecution under the OPA. Although some video versions of films contained scenes that had been cut for theatres (as with Tony Maylam's *The Burning*), other titles such as Lucio Fulci's *House By The Cemetery* and Sam Raimi's *The Evil Dead* were considered impoundable on video in exactly the same format as the BBFC-approved cinema prints. Advising a newsagent whom he had recently acquitted of video obscenity charges, a judge in Wales offered the following advice: 'Remember, if it's dubious, it's *dirty!*' Meanwhile, the director of public prosecutions drew up a list of around 60 actionable titles, which included such bland fare as *The Beyond, Inferno, Terror Eyes, Funhouse, Madhouse, Evilspeak,* and *Visiting Hours.* Ironically, this list, affectionately known to horror fans as 'The Big 60', soon became an indispensable check-list of collectable titles for enthusiasts throughout the country.

Finally in 1984, following a landslide Conservative election victory, the government passed the Video Recordings Act (VRA) under which the BBFC were empowered to classify and cut all video releases with 'special regard to the likelihood of video works...being viewed in the home'. Under these terms, it was tacitly agreed that videos should be judged more harshly than films because they could be rewound, reviewed and thus re-edited at will, and because videos classified for adult viewing only *could* be accessed by children. In 1994, the censorious terms of the VRA were extended by a Criminal Justice Act amendment that instructed the BBFC to be more aware both of the distress caused to young viewers who may view horror videos, and the supposed harm which youths who had viewed such videos may be inspired to wreak upon society. For the BBFC, these legal developments have provided a virtual *carte blanche* for further assaults upon horror cinema in all its forms.

Zombie Flesh Eaters: *'let decency be damned'*

ALAN JONES COLLECTION

Take the case of *The Evil Dead*, director Sam Raimi's gruesomely satirical first feature, which rapidly became a *cause célèbre* both of horror film and video censorship. First submitted to the BBFC in 1983, this violent, slapstick horror-comedy, which specifically strives to elicit a reaction of shocked hilarity from its audience, was granted a theatrical 18 certificate with 40 seconds of cuts, enforced to reduce its 'gross-out' potential. In February 1983, Palace Video released this cut version onto the rental video market, unfortunately coinciding with the rise of press-fuelled hysteria over 'video nasties'. When *The Evil Dead* was finally submitted for a VRA certificate late in 1985, the BBFC banned the title

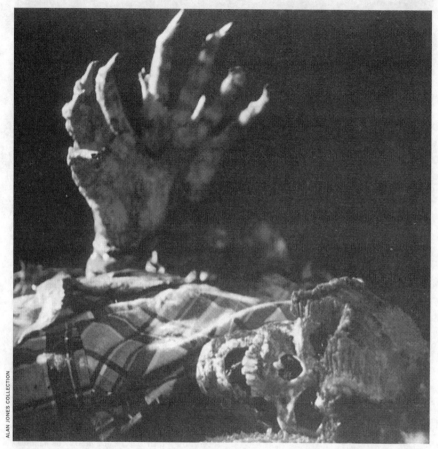

ALAN JONES COLLECTION

The Evil Dead: *violent, slapstick horror comedy the courts found 'obscene'*

outright. According to BBFC deputy director Margaret Ford: 'The Evil Dead has been found obscene in several courts,...[thus] it is incumbent upon us not to pass it, because obviously we would be in breach of our duties to do so.'

Five years later, in 1990, Ferman finally approved a new version of the video, after having cut an additional 65 seconds from seven separate scenes. Rather than cutting any scene in its entirety, the BBFC attempted instead to moderate the video's excessive tone, most notably in their trimming of the notorious 'tree rape' sequence, which remains, but loses its final shot of a branch shooting between the victim's legs. Other cuts

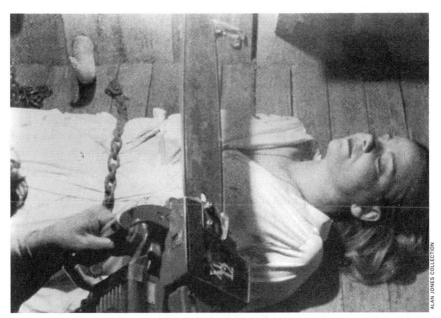

ALAN JONES COLLECTION

The Evil Dead: *'not depraving and corrupting' (James Ferman)*

detailed in the censors' report include: bloody clawing at man's face; zombie's wrist being cut; blood spurting from stump of arm; chopping of a body with an axe (all the former being from one scene); zombie's clawing of a wound in a man's leg which is already bleeding; reduction of man charging into zombie with a wooden post (from the graveside scene). The movie's penultimate climax has also been trimmed, reducing the on-screen disintegration of the demonically possessed youths. This 'significantly different version' arrived on the shelves of British video dealers on 21 May 1990, where it crucially remained open to potential prosecution under the OPA. No such prosecution followed.

What is particularly significant about the BBFC's treatment of *The Evil Dead* is that (despite their proud insistence that they toiled day and night to produce a legal version of a banned horror movie) it pinpoints their inability to respond intelligently (or even consistently) to material whose very purpose is to shock. As Ferman himself has candidly admitted: 'I personally don't think that this film is depraving and corrupting' — the British legal definition of obscenity. So why the cuts?

According to Ferman, he is simply powerless to challenge the verdicts reached by kangaroo courts across the country over a decade ago, verdicts that were themselves clearly affected by the moral panic sweeping Britain in the early 1980s. Nor are the BBFC willing to take a stand against the tabloid press who first fuelled such hysteria, and whose blacklisting of certain titles they clearly know to be unsound. 'The tabloid press are still a symptom of *something*,' Ferman told *Time Out* magazine in 1989. 'They have their fingers on a pulse that people who read *Time Out* and the *Guardian* don't like to acknowledge.'

In 1993, the BBFC sponsored a Policy Studies Institute survey comparing the viewing habits of young offenders with those of random non-offenders. It found no evidence to support allegations of the corruption by video of minors. 'There is not much difference' in what the two groups are watching, reported Tim Newburn of the PSI. 'With reference to horror movies, or movies with a sexual content, or slasher movies...far from being a predominance, there is relatively little evidence that those kids [offenders] are spending much of their time watching them — certainly no more than children of that age generally do.'

But have the findings of the PSI encouraged the BBFC to behave any more leniently toward the horror movies which they now know to be harmless, but which by their very nature contain material which will outrage 'the moral majority'? Not in the slightest. For Ferman, it appears, the BBFC's job is not to assess intelligently whether a horror film or video could deprave or corrupt its likely audience. Rather, it is to mutilate and dilute such material to the point that it would no longer appear outrageous to the tabloid hacks, to make aesthetically palatable that which was designed to offend. Their role is not to protect us from horror movies, but to protect themselves from bad press. For the horror fan, this is business as usual.

Director Sam Raimi reacted with weary resignation to the BBFC's massacring of his acclaimed debut feature. 'The real problem is not *The Evil Dead*,' he sighs, 'the problem is that once the people allow the censors to determine what's right and wrong for them, once they've given them that power, who's to say that a *politically* disturbing film, a picture that differs from the view of the censors *politically*, shouldn't be censored? The people of Britain shouldn't allow them that power, because they'll soon find out that other rights are being taken from them one by one, until they have no right to speak out at all.' ❏

TONY RAYNS

China: censors, scapegoats and bargaining chips

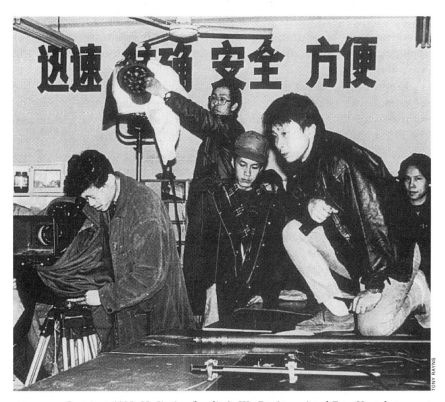

Postman, *1995: He Jianjun (kneeling), Wu Du (camera) and Fang Yuanzheng on set*

TONY RAYNS

Even in the centrally planned days when the Chinese government maintained and paid for a state film industry and expected it to produce hard or soft propaganda, film censorship was a mystery. Decades of Maoist 'purges' had taught Communist bureaucrats never to stick their necks out by taking a defined position — the only exception to this rule being when the bureaucrat was making a calculated bid for greater power — and so processes like censorship were kept deliberately vague and unattributable.

Film censorship was notionally the responsibility of the Film Bureau (then under the aegis of the Ministry of Culture, now under the new Ministry of Radio, Film and Television) but it was never unusual for Film Bureau judgements to be revised or reversed, apparently on orders from higher up. Pinpointing the exact location of a 'blockage' was as impossible as getting a member of the Film Bureau staff to admit to a specific objection to a film. The only person ever held accountable for anything was, of course, the film-maker, who could be blamed for making 'mistakes', paraded as a scapegoat or even forced to retire from the industry.

Ironically, the chaos in China's film industry in 1995 is largely of the Film Bureau's own making. Ever since Deng Xiaoping's 'economic reforms' of 1984, the Film Bureau has been searching for ways to reform the film industry. The overall policy has been to move the industry from the state sector to the private sector, partly to make it more efficient and more responsive to the needs of the audience and partly to eliminate the vast state subsidies that had been propping up the studios. As in all other areas of Chinese public life, though, the shift to a market economy has been compromised at every turn by the government's absolute refusal to relax political controls and by the fact that nothing in the Party's 40-odd years of rule has prepared any film industry personnel for the role of competent management.

Of the 16 feature-film-producing studios in China, only two continue to enjoy direct subsidies from the government: the August 1st Film Studio, owned and run by the People's Liberation Army, and the Children's Film Studio, both in Beijing. The authorities also pay bills for the Central Newsreel and Documentary Studio (which has never been expected to turn a profit), but reputedly at a much lower level than 10 years ago. All other film studios are now expected to stand on their own feet economically. First they had their subsidies withdrawn. Then they

Chungking Express, *1994, director Wong Kar-wai, Hongkong*

'Here, money is law. You hold on less to freedom of expression than to the freedom to make money. So, 1997 means nothing for us. Because Hong Kong is not a cultural space, it is a place, a nowhere. It could be elsewhere. What we expect from China is an enormous market-place... Yes, I could have made more in business, behind a desk. But I live better as I live. There's nothing as fun as the cinema.'

Kirk Wong, Hong Kong director of Crime Story *and* Rock 'n' Roll Cop

(Quoted in *Le Monde*)

The Blue Kite, *1993: 'homage to a generation'*

were told to stop expecting unlimited credit at the Bank of China. And then they were told to start distributing their own productions in China, and to take responsibility for selling them abroad. At the same time, in response to pressure from Jack Valenti of the US Motion Picture Producers Association (MPPA), the authorities cautiously began opening the China market to American distributors. The vanguard title in Chinese release this year, appropriately enough, was James Cameron's *True Lies*.

Beijing Film Studio and Shanghai Film Studio — the country's largest — responded to these changes in three ways. First, by abandoning all their own plans for production and devolving production to a number of quasi-autonomous 'private' companies within the studio. (Most of these 'private' companies are headed by well-known directors — Xie Jin in Shanghai, Tian Zhuangzhuang in Beijing — whose names are expected to attract outside investment.) Second, by going into joint-venture productions with the new, genuinely private, film companies springing up in China's cities, most of them offshoots of real-estate and investment finance companies. And third, by turning their studios into service centres for relatively well-funded productions from Hong Kong, Taiwan and elsewhere.

The other studios, ranging from medium-sized operations like those in Changchun and Xi'an to the tiny regional outposts in places like Nanning, Changsha and Chengdu, didn't have most of those options. Massively overstaffed, carrying exorbitant overheads and incompetently managed, they are floundering along trying to stave off bankruptcy. Xi'an Film Studio, which still has loose ties with bankable directors like Huang Jianxin, Zhou Xiaowen and He Ping, thanks to its glory days under Wu Tianming in the 1980s, has managed to attach itself to a number of privately financed movies and looks likely to survive. But most of the others will have disappeared before the end of the decade. Amid this chaos, the processes of censorship have become more elusive than ever. As if to compensate for its diminished role in the film industry, the Film Bureau routinely demands minor changes in the finished films it vets for release at home and abroad, even when the film differs in no visible way from its pre-approved script. The cutting of foreign films brought into China legally for theatrical or video release has become increasingly capricious and unpredictable. New and byzantine regulations have been brought in to control the films shot in China by overseas Chinese directors, especially those from Hong Kong; but where Clara Law (who now divides her time between Hong Kong and Melbourne) has been 'blacklisted' for smuggling erotic material past the censors for her feature *Temptation of a Monk*, other Hong Kong directors (no names, no pack-drill) have done exactly the same thing with complete impunity.

No case better illustrates the Film Bureau's current mix of mercenary pragmatism and political control than its treatment of Zhang Yimou. Zhang has always been especially vulnerable to official disapproval because (unlike his contemporaries Chen Kaige and Tian Zhuangzhuang) he comes from what the Communist party defines as a 'bad class background'; he has lived with the risk of arbitrary punishment or victimisation all his life. At the same time, his spectacular international success with films like *Ju Dou* (1991) and *Raise the Red Lantern* (1992) marked him out as a prime target for official recuperation. Zhang began working for overseas producers (who offered him better pay, higher technical standards and some measure of protection from the vagaries of the Film Bureau) in 1990, right after the Tiananmen Square massacre, and 1994's *To Live* was his fourth feature in succession to be owned by a company outside China.

Clearly recognising that the only way to save China's film industry from terminal decline was to get internationally successful directors like Zhang back working for it, the Film Bureau made *To Live* a scapegoat film. No specific cuts or changes were demanded, but the Film Bureau made plain that it had strong objections to the film. (It has not to this day authorised its release in China.) Zhang Yimou was sufficiently intimidated by this to cancel his intended visit to 1994's Cannes Film Festival, where the film was premiered by its Hong Kong producer. And when his next project, *Shanghai Triad*, scheduled to be made for French producers, was cancelled on the eve of production, it proved relatively easy to further intimidate Zhang into agreeing to make a revised version of the film for Shanghai Film Studio instead.

Since the French had already pre-sold *Shanghai Triad* to distributors around the world, the Chinese authorities allowed them to retain the international sales rights. But the Film Bureau had succeeded in bringing Zhang himself back under control. In the future, he must make films for China's studios, which will own them and hence make profits from them. The Film Bureau, meanwhile, will retain full censorship control of the films. No Zhang Yimou film in the immediate future will be allowed out of China on any terms without specific Film Bureau approval. Given these circumstances, it is of course not surprising that Zhang made *Shanghai Triad* as such a politically safe and crowd-pleasing movie.

Phase Two of the authorities' plan to recuperate 'problem' film-makers has been their approval of Tian Zhuangzhuang's quasi-private production company within Beijing Film Studio. The Film Bureau was livid when it failed to prevent the completion and international release of Tian's *The Blue Kite*, a film financed from Hong Kong and Japan which remains banned in China because Tian made radical departures from the approved script. Then, when Tian resigned from his 'work unit' to become self-employed, the Film Bureau retaliated by blacklisting him: no studio, company or individual was permitted to finance or work with him. The 'work unit' in question, Beijing Film Studio, was given its best chance yet of surviving and prospering when Han Sanping was appointed its new head in the spring of 1995. A man of the same age as the 'Fifth Generation' film-makers, Han made it his first priority to get Tian de-

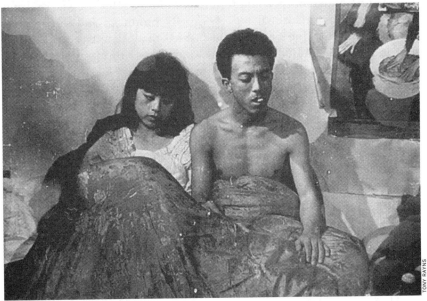

Top: Filming The Days, 1993 Wang Xiaoshuai (centre) director
Below: Yu Hong and Liu Xiaodong, starring

blacklisted. Tian was at first deeply suspicious of Han's efforts on his behalf, but eventually agreed to rejoin the studio as a producer and was given Film Bureau clearance to do so. Tian's new position is much less compromised than Zhang Yimou's, but he too is now back with China's domestic film industry.

As a producer, Tian Zhuangzhuang's policy has been to give career breaks to new directors, especially those who have graduated from the Beijing Film Academy (China's only real film school), but been unable to get a job with any of the studios. The most striking development in the Chinese cinema of the last five years has been the appearance of unauthorised independent films and videotapes by these same directors. Their films and tapes, made without official permission or control, are the first to emerge from China since the Communists took power in 1949. Tian's attempts to produce new films by these directors represents not a back-door way of bringing them under state control (although everybody accepts that it will have that side-effect) but a way of retrieving them from the poverty of means which is endemic among independent film-makers the world over.

The first of the independent features was *Mama* (1990), conceived and set up by Wang Xiaoshuai but eventually produced and directed by Zhang Yuan when the Film Bureau insisted that Wang take up a junior post in Fujian Film Studio. The film was privately financed on the back of the UN Year of the Child; it centres on a woman separated from her husband who tries to hold down her job as a librarian while also looking after her retarded teenage son without help from the authorities. Zhang Yuan (a graduate from the cinematography department of the Beijing Film Academy) intersperses the story with documentary material — glimpses of real retarded children in care, interviews with their parents and other carers — and grounds the fictional material in a realistic sense of grass-roots' lives in Beijing of a kind never seen in mainland Chinese cinema before. On completion, the film was sold to the Xi'an Film Studio, which put its logo on the front, but the Film Bureau nonetheless banned it from distribution in China. A copy was smuggled to Hong Kong, from where the film began circulating internationally. The Film Bureau finally cleared *Mama* for release in China in 1993, but remains angry that the film was sent abroad without its approval.

Mama, however, inaugurated a small torrent of independently made films and tapes. By 1993, Wang Xiaoshuai had quit his post in Fujian and made his debut feature, *The Days,* on privately raised capital of approximately US$7,000. He Jianjun (also known as He Yi), who had worked as a continuity assistant on films by Chen Kaige and Zhang Yimou and made a few experimental short films, had similarly rustled up some US$10,000 to make his debut feature, *Red Beads.* Zhang Yuan had gone on from *Mama* to make a series of music videos for China's rock pioneer Cui Jian; these led directly into his second feature, *Beijing Bastards,* starring Cui Jian and dealing with the confused and directionless kids who use Cui's music as the soundtrack to their lives. At the same time, video-documentary director Wu Wenguang was shooting tapes about the lives of self-employed artists in Beijing while ex–TV directors Wen Pulin and Duan Jinchuan were shooting engaged and highly respectful tapes about the Buddhist philosophies and traditions of Tibet. Also circulating underground were anonymous tapes about Beijing's students in the aftermath of the Tiananmen Square massacre.

All these films and tapes have one thing in common beyond the fact that they were made 'illegally' in the eyes of the Film Bureau: they all spring from their makers' desires to deal with aspects of their own lives and experiences that they found either missing from or misrepresented by the state's official art and broadcast media. *The Days* offers a piercingly truthful account of the psychological and emotional problems besetting China's impoverished urban intellectuals in the 1990s; *Red Beads* constructs a tragi-comic metaphor for young people's struggles to stay sane while rejecting the tenets of traditional (Confucian) morality. The fiction films also share a remarkably frank and matter-of-fact attitude to questions of sexual behaviour and identity; this alone would be enough to guarantee banning by the Film Bureau if the films had been financed and produced within the system.

The Film Bureau's first direct action against the independents was to bring pressure on the financier of Zhang Yuan's third feature, *Chicken Feathers on the Ground.* The man was sufficiently frightened to halt the production less than a week after it started; it eventually resumed as an approved project with a different director. (The abrupt curtailment of the original shoot and the consequent discussions were documented by Zhang Yuan's wife Ning Dai in her tape *A Film is Stopped.*) Then in March 1994, after Zhang Yuan, Ning Dai and Wang Xiaoshuai had attended the Rotterdam Film Festival with their work, the Film Bureau issued its notorious blacklist, proscribing six named individuals and one

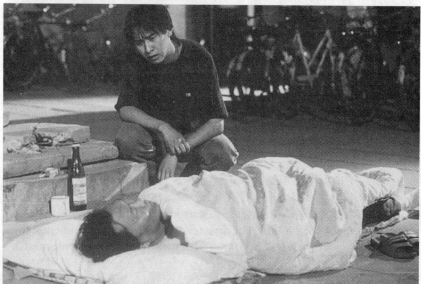

Filming Sons, *1995*
Top: Zhang Yuan (centre) director
Below: Still from Sons

video collective from producing further 'illegal' films and tapes.

Encouragingly, the only visible effect of the blacklist has been to spur the independent film-makers to greater creative heights. Zhang Yuan's riposte to the Film Bureau was to make *The Square*, an observational documentary about Tiananmen Square — not only the most public space in the whole of China but also the country's symbolic heart. Zhang is now completing a docu-drama called *Sons*, dealing with the real-life relationship between a mentally unstable alcoholic and his two drop-out sons, and plans to go on to make a feature about Beijing's gay subculture. He Jianjun completed his second feature *Postman*, poised as acutely as *Red Beads* between black comedy and tragedy, dealing with the elusive status of privacy in Chinese society. Wang Xiaoshuai has also shot a second feature, as yet unedited, and the cinematographer Wu Di directed *Goldfish*, a comedy drama about the desire (widespread among young people in China's cities) to emigrate. And underground video production continues to proliferate.

It says a lot about the lawlessness prevailing in China today that the Film Bureau's blacklist was unable to put a stop to independent film and video-making. In the China of the mid-1990s, it is always possible to find an official who will turn a blind eye to some infraction of the rules in return for a modest kickback, or a company that will provide a service for a 'blacklisted' client if the client has ready cash to spend. More intriguing is the Film Bureau's evident reluctance to act directly against the independent film-makers by, for example, rescinding their passports or taking them to court for flouting censorship and export regulations. The wild card in play seems to be the fact that the independent films and tapes have been exported and warmly received around the world. This apparently deters the Film Bureau from jumping on the film-makers as other sections of the Chinese government have jumped on human rights activists, labour activists, dissident writers and others. The international visibility of the films and tapes directly protects the people who made them. The more people who see films like *Beijing Bastards* and *Postman*, the more valuable the films become as bargaining chips in the struggle for a genuine freedom of expression in China. ❏

TIAN ZHUANGZHUANG

History...homage...memory

Filming was a nightmare from the outset [in December 1991].
Anonymous letters acccusing us of 'opposing the Communist Party
and Socialism' were sent to the Party Central Committee as well as the
Ministry of Broadcasting. The latter wanted to stop shooting but it was
referred up to the Ministry of Propaganda and, in the end, nothing
happened. Then, when we'd finished shooting, the anonymous letters
started again: the studio banned post-production in Japan and I couldn't
complete it. A year later, with the help of a Dutch company it was
completed and premiered in Cannes at the 1993 festival. The publicity
got back to China, the government boycotted the Tokyo film festival
[where *The Blue Kite* won prizes for best film and best actress] and
prevented me from leaving the country.

I eventually got myself 'released' from the Beijing Film Studio and
that particular problem is over now that I'm no longer a part of any
official institution. But the film still can't be shown in China.

After *Horse Thief* (1986) had taken eight months to get through the
censors, I just made whatever came along: it didn't seem worth fighting.

I never set out to make newspaper headlines; but I did know making
the film I wanted would create huge problems for me and the people
who would have to pass it. Despite other offers of work, I had to make
The Blue Kite: telling this story had become an obsession. On reaching
my 40s, I found myself more and more thinking about the past, China's
history since the Revolution. Our parents' generation paid for this
history with their blood and tears. Politics trampled everything else
underfoot — human nature, dignity, warmth, personal affection. If
China really wants to change, people have to understand what's
happened, get rid of the idea that politics rules their lives.

Many people today don't know anything about this period.
Discussion of the persecutions of the anti-Rightist campaign that
followed the 'hundred flowers' policy is still taboo for writers, artists and
film-makers. The mistakes, hardships and persecution of other mass

movements — the Great Leap Forward followed by economic chaos and famine in which millions starved, the Cultural Revolution with its witch-hunt of class enemies — were all part of a single historical flow. They tore into ordinary people, broke up families like a distant hurricane. *The Blue Kite* pays homage to my parents' generation.

I was born in 1952. A lot of what happens in the film is based on my memories and things my father and people of his generation told me later. My parents were both Party cadres. The stories are real. But it is precisely this very fear of reality that prevents such stories being told.

There are too many films that have nothing to do with reality: heroic epics, comedies, farces, kung fu and so on. I'm not putting them down, but film isn't just about entertainment. History has to be told as we understand and remember it. We can't leave it to the next generation; they're more interested in rock and roll than what happened to their parents. It's the first time this period has been shown from this perspective, through the eye of the child I was. It's frightening and confusing: living through 'history' is like that. *The Blue Kite* is made in compassion for a generation that suffered and in the hope that the next generation won't repeat the same things. It gives them a memory they have been denied — by the Party and by the young themselves, who simply want to get on with the business of catching up with the West.

Interview by Judith Vidal-Hall

JOHN BOORMAN

Beyond Rangoon

In 1988, the largely student-led Campaign for Democracy in Burma was brutally crushed by the military dictatorship. Thousands of students were massacred, many more fled into the jungles of the north. The army terrorised the nation. Millions of people were displaced. Refugees poured over the border into Thailand.

Burma was a country closed off from the world. No foreign journalists were allowed in. Consequently, the extent of the horror was largely concealed from the rest of the world. *Beyond Rangoon* set about reconstructing these terrible events that had gone unrecorded. We shot the movie in Malaysia where Tony Pratt, the designer, brilliantly reproduced Burma.

The State Law and Order Council (SLORC), the Burmese dictatorship, campaigned to stop the picture being made and almost succeeded. The Malaysians withdrew all co-operation and threatened to expel us. We hung on by faking up a script that did not mention Burma.

Burmese democracy groups in exile used the release of the film in 1995 as a focus for their campaign. Screenings were arranged for politicians in London, Paris and Washington.

Six years after the uprising, thousands of political prisoners remained in jail including the charismatic leader, Aung San Suu Kyi. Shortly before the US opening of the film, she was unexpectedly released. She expressed the view that the film had been a factor in SLORC's decision.

The conventional wisdom in Hollywood is that political films are box-office poison, and so it proved with *Beyond Rangoon*. It failed to find a mass audience. The woes of the world are thrust upon us at home through television news. I suppose people look to the movies as a refuge from reality. However, I know from the letters I got from across the world that many people were deeply affected by the film and asked what they could do to help. I had a similar response to *The Emerald Forest*, people wanting to know what they could do to help save the rain forests. In both cases I put them in touch with pressure groups, and some people have been thus politicised.

Truth has a witness...

CASTLE ROCK

I believe that movies exercise considerable influence over the young, mostly bad. Given the movies that dominate our screens it would be hard to argue otherwise. Given the world we have, should we expect more?

But now and then it happens. A film comes along that gives an insight into a place, a nation, a community, that affirms our common humanity. And very occasionally there is a popular joyful response and our faith in film is restored.

ROMAN POLANSKI

A matter of perception

'There is no absolute evil, no single truth; everything's relative.' Ever since seeing *Rashomon* many years ago, the multiple vision — 'there are more than two sides to every story' — has been an important element in Roman Polanski's work. As has the naturalism that results from studied precision and perfection with the camera. 'I fought for realism from the beginning. I wanted to make death dirty, like it is; involve people in the guilt. Not the clean, tidy death in 1960s US movies. Death is squalid: no grand gestures.' He cites the 'real' violence confronting us daily: the terrible, unheroic images from former-Yugoslavia and Rwanda today; Vietnam and Cambodia earlier. And, like many, sees the real villain in TV, the great 'mixer', that makes entertainment out of real-life drama and confuses the outcome of both. 'Look at the O J Simpson soap': and mimicks the swirling theme tune and 'designer graphics' that introduce each episode.

Mood, atmosphere is important: claustrophobia, fear, tightly contained within the rigours of the classic unities. It's the menace, the imminent threat of disaster, and the sudden, unexpected 'always just a little before you expect it' shock of violence, more than excess of the real thing that have earned the reputation.

Violence is 'the world we live in' and evil's no more than 'what you think is evil'. A startling assertion from someone who saw the rest of his family disappear into Nazi concentration camps, his mother for ever, when he was around eight years old and who himself survived the Krakow ghetto only by disappearing into the hostile and precarious security of a primitive Catholic Polish countryside. Other events in the life seem no less absolute: like the bizarre and brutal murder of wife and unborn child by the Manson gang in Los Angeles in 1969.

But he persists. We don't talk about World War II Poland, but neither apartheid nor torture and disappearances in Latin America change the dictum. 'Depends where you're standing, the angle of vision. Apartheid wasn't evil to the guys who were winning...'

This multi-faceted vision, the refusal to subscribe to clear-cut categories — victim/victimiser, good/evil, light/dark, guilt/innocence — the membrane separating victim and tormentor is porous — has much to do with the success of the latest film, *Death and the Maiden*, a tight, claustrophobic thriller in which suspense and the shadow of a doubt are sustained to the last shot. Even beyond. The end remains as ambiguous as the opening shots. As the film develops against the background of a violent storm, a power failure puts out the light and cuts off communication with the outside world. In semi-darkness, the camera cuts between the three protagonists, becoming, in turn, the champion of each: the tortured wife, the eminent human rights lawyer commissioned to examine events under the dictatorship — but not all of them — and the good Samaritan doctor whom the wife believes to be her tormentor. Each has a version of events, an angle on the truth.

Based on the play by Chilean writer Ariel Dorfman, *Death and the Maiden* is a tale of crime, punishment and forgiveness; retribution and reconciliation. Reconciliation/retribution, suggest the film-maker, are two sides of the same coin. There is no forgiveness: we go on living, tormentor and victim, in daily proximity.

Even in Communist Poland, where his first feature, *Knife in the Water*, ran foul of the censors for avoiding a politically correct

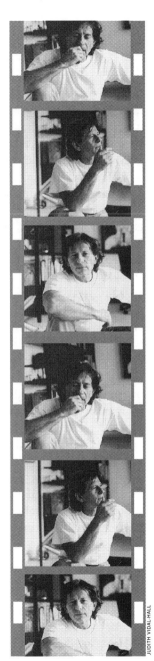

JUDITH VIDAL-HALL

resolution, Polanski has steered clear of any obvious political engagement. So why the Dorfman, an obviously *engagé* piece of work? 'Apart from the fact that I loved its enclosed, claustrophobic character, it's about human rights, guilt and responsibility in society. How you deal with the past. Even if you agree that Paulina [the wife] is right and that Miranda [the doctor] is guilty, you still have a problem. Do you deal with those people in the same way they dealt with you? It's all over the world: the old Communist countries for instance. Poland has had so many changes, censorship made a travesty of our history since the beginning of World War II: so many histories untold; so many blank spaces.'

Polanski, too, has a lot of past to deal with. Forgive? 'Never. Forget. That's the only way people can go on living together in a society.' And he has made it quite clear in the autobiography, *Roman by Polanski*, that that is how he personally handles the horrors. At a deep, uncombed subterranean level they may inform his films; the latter are not autobiography.

More than any other film-maker, Polanski has been dogged by the confusion of life and art. Critics, to his justifiable irritation, constantly cross-dress the personal life and public work. And, as always, the pundits want it both ways: after the brutal murder of his second wife, Sharon Tate, by the Manson group, it was a case of 'if a man makes films like that' — with the then recently released *Rosemary's Baby* in mind — 'then of course he courts such macabre happenings.' On the other hand, 'with an experience like that behind him and the childhood, no wonder he makes the films he does.' The conviction and imprisonment for statutory rape in 1977 completed the circle and compounded the myth to the satisfaction of outsiders.

No need to talk about the life; here's the man. 'I know what I am, what I've done and haven't done.' Eighteen years' exile in Paris have rooted the hobgoblin in something solid: marriage and a child. He bounces in on sprung sneakers, jeans and a monogrammed tee-shirt, clearly bored at the prospect of another interview. Polanski is about as accomplished an actor as he is director. A pose is easily assumed, until a new direction engages a questing mind, still, with child-like curiosity, searching for answers to some of the harder questions.

As the man who more or less reinvented the genre that hovers on the murky border between violence and horror with *Repulsion* (1968), Polanski has been pursued by a reputation for gratuitous violence, a favourite target of the victims of moral panic and censors who watch the fine detail in expectation. Even *Chinatown*, considered his masterpiece and one of the finest pieces of film-making in modern cinema, has been thus tagged. It is a complex, densely plotted thriller with a Chandler/Hammett look-alike private eye played by Jack Nicholson, and set in 1930s LA. Its subject matter is corruption and incest; the political and personal violence that characterises both. Polanski jump cuts from clock-watching boredom to extreme animation. This is something he knows about; really knows. He savages the myth of power as much as the absurdity of the censorship it drags in its wake, and cries foul at the would-be censors of *Chinatown*.

'Something very subtle goes on in front of the camera, it's about feelings, emotion: something happening in the eye — camera, actor, audience. Those tyrants, Nazi, Communist, knew that.' Reflectively. Then bursts out, 'We're talking here as though cinema were an abstract power; something separate from life, acting on its own. I just don't believe that. Nothing has the power of reality.' And he relates how, after watching *Schindler's List*, he got in a whole lot of post-World War II documentary footage on the camps and ghettos of the Third Reich for the benefit of his much younger French wife who knew little of the history. 'I had a sister, Annette. She died not long ago. One day, soon after seeing all this stuff, Emmanuelle, my wife, said to her, "That's funny, I sometimes write telephone numbers on my arm like you." She had no idea what she was seeing. Even after all those films, it just wasn't real until that moment. That's power — reality.

'And you can't have it both ways,' he insists. 'If cinema doesn't have that sort of power, then the arguments of the censors — corruptor of children, copy-cat crimes, the instigator of violence and horror — won't work either. 'Fuck the censors. They're preposterous; an imposition on society. Who the hell do they think they are telling me what I can read or see? Who are these people who are allowed to watch all this? What do you do with them at the end? Lock them up in an insane asylum? Put them in prison because they've become a danger to society or to themselves? Or should we give them compensation for exposing themselves to images, like we do to people who get exposed to radiation?'

But above all it's 'absurd'. Censorship ends up locking people into darkened rooms. Another anecdote. In his biography, Polanski describes how the boy Romek was, from very young, passionate about cinema. Most of the time that meant surmounting barriers of one kind or another to watch the forbidden fruit. Often simply to overcome the lack of money. Under the Nazis, for the escapee from the Krakow ghetto, that meant the Aryan joys of Leni Riefenstahl —'Oh, they were so beautiful those films' — in the early Communism, the odd delight from Hollywood or the best in Soviet propaganda. 'One day, when we finally got as far as the door to the auditorium, we found it locked! My God, they had locked the audience in so they couldn't leave until they'd seen the whole thing!' Positive propaganda; positive uncensorship. 'What the Polish censors didn't like about *Knife in the Water* was the lack of a positive message. Send the wrongdoers to prison, or make them confess the whole thing at the nearest police station, they suggested.' Attempts to protect the European film industry by imposing quotas on US films would also, he laughed, now in fine humour, 'end up by locking French audiences into French films'.

It's a lot of effort to get up and go out to the cinema, he says, and if you get yourself together to do just that, a little plaintively, people should leave alone. When it comes to video 'that I bring back into the privacy of my home, it's no different from censoring books in the public library.'

'Television', he concedes, looking at the handsome set in a room of the large Avenue Montaigne flat that serves as office and home, 'could be a little bit different. It's only a piece of furniture but it talks to you, confronts you with images without warning.' And yes, as a recent father of a two-and-a-half-year-old daughter, Morgane, he's thought about the great excuse, the 'it's all to protect the children' argument. Of course the sensibilities of children must be protected from the most violent images. 'But because my daughter doesn't like storms doesn't mean we shouldn't ever film storms. Children are to a great degree self-regulating in what they watch, and more resilient than we think in dealing with their fears.'

As for adults, in France, 'we have explicit sex in all possible combinations on TV, and nobody's harmed.' Adding, and not for the first time, 'It's only in Britain you have this problem.' It's not the only time he refers to the peculiarity of Anglo-Saxon attitudes. Maybe confession is the answer, proffers the Jew to the English? As for the USA, 'it's all about rating certificates, distribution, who'll take the film and what's the marketing going to be like; there's no censorship as such.'

As to *Chinatown*, critics, including the head of Paramount at the time,

BFI STILLS

Chinatown, 1974: now you see it, now you don't

who howl about too much blood, 'don't know what they've seen'. Like Newton on optics, or Einstein on relativity, Polanski has a general theory on violence in the movies. 'There are three elements that amplify our perception of violence: we've identified with the character (who is killed in the last frame of the film), invested a lot of emotion in her, it's a shock when she dies. Then, the entire film was very realistically made, it looks, you know, truthful, the details, the acting, the use of the camera. There's not much blood but what there is is authentic. And, you know, it's not so much what you see as what you imagine you see.' And he quotes from Richard Gregory's *Eye and Brain*, as he did years ago in the autobiography, and now, precisely, from memory: 'Gregory says our perceptions are shaped by the sum of our visual experiences. We see far less than we think we see because of past impressions stored in our mind. When people came out from *Rosemary's Baby*, they were convinced they'd seen the baby, cloven hooves and all. All they'd really seen, for a split second, was a subliminal superimposition of the catlike eyes...We perceive much less that we imagine we do.' But wait a minute; can the millions be that wrong? He insists: it's the baggage we carry around. 'Violence is the world we live in.'

Not that anything much is left to the imagination by the new boys like Tarantino or even veterans like Oliver Stone. 'It's all terribly explicit now but it's less effective. I fought for reality and look where it's got to. A little blood goes a long way. I hate all this blood splashing around the screen. It looks phoney, unreal, almost a spoof. Because we haven't invested anything in these characters, the only shock is in the violence, not an assault on the emotions.' But he concedes that the world changes and it's a lot to do with style. 'The language of cinema has changed. There's a new grammar, more pace.' Like literature. 'We wouldn't, after all,' he asks, 'expect a novel of the late twentieth century to read like Zola or Dickens, would we now?'

Jack Nicholson said of him, 'That little Polish bastard is one goddam genius,' adding, 'whatever anyone says about his private life, I know he's never hurt a living soul.' The bright-eyed, half-starved on pickled gherkins, greedy for life and grasping at every sensory experience kid from the ghetto has also been called 'the finest movie director in the modern era'. That was John Huston. Nothing if not controversial, the man whom others — and he quotes — have called 'that evil little dwarf', slowly comes into focus in the no-man's land where victim and victimiser meet. Suddenly you know who he is: little Oscar, the boy with the tin drum who refused to grow until the grown-ups put their world to rights. Brilliant fantasies and 'too much reality'.

He denies reports that he's about to make a World War II movie in Poland, or even has plans to go back there. 'The haemorrhage of talent from Poland was worse than anywhere. The decay is physical as well as mental.' The 'great expectations' he observed on his visit there in 1981 have subsided; he wasn't at all sure that the situation in the film industry was easily reversible. He spoke about his 'beloved' Mikhail Bulgakov (*Index* 8/1991), the uncompromising Russian master of the surreal, and author of *The Master and Margarita*.

Rich in irony, ambiguity and with flights of fantasy unsurpassed in twentieth-century literature, now there's a challenge for a man whose first film, *Two Men and a Wardrobe*, was, they say, a miniature masterpiece of the surreal. So much for realism. ❏

Interview by Judith Vidal-Hall

AÍDA BORTNIK

A gamble against oblivion

I've never accepted either in my profession or my life 'the official version' of anything. As a writer, I learned to take nothing for granted: not only must one write, one must not stay silent. Throughout history, words have created the memory of humanity fighting against oblivion.

In 1972 I wrote and directed my first play, *Soldiers*. A series of songs and monologues representing the universal and timeless symbols of peoples, weapons, war and repression. The theatre was packed from the opening night; then as later, Argentina was ruled by the military. Every performance included a 'quartet' of persistent spectators whom we knew were military intelligence and who soberly 'recorded' every face in the audience.

We were young and naive; at the time we had no idea that the present dictatorship was no more than a dress rehearsal for the horror that was to come. The challenge provoked us. How far could I go?

Since then, that gamble with fortune became my true language: the language that defeats the censors but audiences recognise.

In 1974, my first screenplay, *The Truce* (a free adaptation of Mario Benedetti's novel), became the first Spanish-language film to be nominated for an Oscar. On the surface, it was only the story of a widower in his late 50s, father of three, lonely and dignified, who falls in love with a girl his daughter's age.

Years later we learnt the film was taken as a 'model' of 'hidden subversion'. For actor Hector Alterio, who played the leading role, it meant threats and exile. I became even more 'undesirable' for the ultra-right groups that emerged in 1975. Only a year later, after the *coup d'état* in March 1976, those same groups became synonymous with the organised repression of government.

The following May, *Cuestionario*, the magazine on which I worked, was threatened. Since *Cuestionario* refused to submit to censorship, and I was already 'blacklisted', when the magazine itself became a *desaparecido* I could no longer work. They banned all my work retrospectively: none of my television scripts, plays or screenplays could be seen.

I had just finished a film version of Haroldo Conti's *Around the Cage*. Conti was a professor of literature and a wonderful writer; one of the most noble and vital men I ever knew. Two days after we had finished work on the script, an armed group burst into his house and, in front of

his wife and children, destroyed everything, including the manuscript he was working on. They took him away to torture and death. There was never any reply to international appeals on his behalf; his body was never identified.

Two months after Conti became yet another *desaparecido*, I took a cargo ship to Spain. Hector Alterio was already there. Three years later, still in exile, I saw the film. It could only mean Haroldo was dead and ended any hope that I would be able to return.

Yet, only three months later, I was asked to return to Buenos Aires for a month to collaborate on a film of my story *The Island*. Unable to control either fear or temptation, in four days' time and with a small bag, I returned home. It took only 24 hours to decide I was never going back into exile.

The Island was my only attempt at a 'metaphorical film'. The characters are 'sick people' in a psychiatric institute, and 'healthy relatives' who visit them with a mixture of guilt and fear. The project escaped censorship, but the audience in Argentina and abroad knew what it was about. It was the only Argentine film to receive international awards during the dictatorship.

In 1982, the Malvinas war was beginning to undermine the regime and I was again a recipient of threatening and increasingly violent telephone calls. A TV mini-series, written between two prohibition periods, provoked the wrath of my admirers. But I already had a taste of the liberty to come and was writing what would later be *The Official Story* [UK title *The Official Version*].

The Official Story (1985), the first film to confront the reality of the seven years of the last dictatorship, allowed me to exorcise these and other demons. Writing it from the point of view of someone who had managed to ignore what had gone on meant seeing not through the eyes of victim or victimiser, but with those of that huge majority which, late as ever, would discover it had been both things.

At the beginning we thought of filming it in Spain; but history began to exceed our wildest dreams. *The Official Story* was the first film shot in the new democracy. It changed the lives of those who worked on it. But it had already changed mine before it was shot. Writing it had freed me. Seeing my beloved friend Hector Alterio return to Argentina to play the leading role made me feel the

HISTORIAS CINEMATOGRÁFICAS

Poster for The Official Story, 1985: an indictment of silence

nightmare was really over. Not undamaged, but whole. The Mothers of the Plaza de Mayo wrote of it: 'The Official Story is a conscience-shaking indictment of the seven years of military dictatorship during which many, from terror or self-preservation, kept silent, pretending to ignore what was going on.'

Writing is an attempt to remind people that staying human is a far bigger adventure than mere survival. As well as a gamble against oblivion. ❏

Political encounters

BFI STILLS

Bogart and Bacall: holding the line against McCarthy

JONATHAN FOREMAN

Foreman and Churchill discuss the film Young Winston, *1965*

Witch-hunt

Oscar-winning director Carl Foreman was an early victim of the informers and blacklisters who rampaged through Hollywood during McCarthy's witch hunt. His son recalls a loyal citizen and man of high principle

My father used to kid us, with just a hint of wistfulness, about being 'my English children', as if after 20-odd years of exile he was still slightly amazed to have this English family and English life. It was an unexpected second act to the personal catastrophe of being blacklisted. The fact that my sister and I were there at all, twittering away in our foreign accents, was a reminder of the career and the life that had been cut off by the Hollywood Inquisition, and the price he had paid for refusing to name names.

By all accounts, during the course of this new life in London, he eventually became a happier man than he had ever been, going on to break the blacklist in 1957 and remarrying in 1964. Yet there was always a bitterness, an anger rippling below the surface. I think it was one of the reasons he didn't move back to the USA until the collapse of the British film industry in 1975. In the beginning of his time away, the anger was overwhelming. For the first year or so in England, for all his determination not to play a martyr's role, he actually found he couldn't write; every time he sat down at a typewriter, all that came out was the beginning of a furious letter to the *New York Times*.

But once we did move back it was hard to avoid bumping into the informers and blacklisters who were still around, some of them, like Ronald Reagan, claiming that the blacklist had never existed. Hollywood never really came clean and those who had been part of the blacklist machine never apologised for the pointless humiliation of people who have never plotted treason or sabotage, for making hundreds of people ritually betray their colleagues and friends, for the destruction of scores of careers, or for the collaboration with a Congressional Committee that trampled the Constitution in a cynical and sadistic bid for publicity.

I remember once, when I was about 10, being with my father in an elevator of an office building in LA. A man in late middle age walked in and, seeing my father, put out his hand and said, 'Hello Carl'. My father didn't say a word. He gripped my shoulder painfully hard and marched us both out of the open door. His face was white with anger. I had never seen my generally genial father ever say or do anything rude before, and I asked him why he hadn't said hello. He explained that the man was one of several people who had named him before the Committee. He didn't bother to tell me the man's name. It was hard for me to understand, at the time, why he couldn't just be nice and say hello anyway. After all, the hearings had been a long time ago.

I came to see that the whole blacklist experience deepened his sense, born during the Depression, that success, or rather security, of any kind was terribly fragile. He even maintained small bank accounts in five or six countries around the world, as if he half expected things to fall apart again. And he was adamant that his children should be members of a profession other than his own.

I think it was because of his experiences that we grew up with a heightened, even exaggerated sense of the importance of loyalty. I remember my surprise, as a boarder at prep school (a situation wholly alien to his own experience), when he wholeheartedly approved of the schoolboy code that made 'sneaking' on another boy unacceptable. His contempt for 'stool pigeons' was almost boundless.

While he could understand, if not forgive, those who had informed on him and others, there were some betrayals that went beyond understanding. In 1951, with *High Noon* about to go into production, his best friend and partner, Stanley Kramer, on hearing that Carl had been subpoenaed by the House Un-American Activities Committee (HUAC), tried to kick him out of the company they had founded together. I gained insight into his resulting feelings about treachery — and the limits of group solidarity — when, as a teenager, I came across E M Forster's famous quotation: 'If I had to choose between betraying my country or my friend, I hope I should have the guts to betray my country.' At the time, I thought it was a wonderful sentiment, and said so to my father. Given what I knew about what had happened to him, and his views on informers, it never occurred to me that he would almost shout at me, telling me he thought it disgusting, self-indulgent nonsense. Think what it means, he said. To betray one's fellow countrymen, millions of trusting strangers, was monstrous.

I had not realised until then how much his country meant to him, and though I knew he had never even considered giving up his citizenship, I had misunderstood his visceral scorn for informers. His defiance of the Committee had not merely been a matter of loyalty to friends and colleagues — it was a matter of principle.

Of course, by the time I was born he had come to love the country that allowed him to stay and work and also restored his sense of dignity. He was very conscious of the ironies of the situation: an American going to England to be free, sailing from New York on the *Liberté*, being deprived of his passport by a Democrat secretary of state on 4 July 1953, at an American Armed Forces football game in Wembley Stadium, only to be given informal asylum by the staff of a Conservative home secretary. Nonetheless like most (though not all) Americans who had passed through the Communist Party during the Depression or the World War II, he was an American first. For all that had been done to him and others, and for all that he disapproved of wars fought to maintain corrupt and brutal dictatorships, he was proud of America's ideals.

Hollywood had changed during Carl Foreman's years away, although it hadn't become a community noted for courage or introspection or honesty. Many of the traits that made the industry so vulnerable when HUAC rode into town were still there. It was as provincial and cut off from real politics as ever, while its glamour still brought publicity-hungry politicians out to the coast for Hollywood-bashing. There was still a skin-deep liberalism, a half-baked radicalism being loudly proclaimed by people, many of whom felt vaguely guilty about the amount of money they were making. And an ugly, dumb super-patriotism that searched for the enemy within.

In some quarters it has become fashionable again to deride the victims of the Hollywood blacklist, as if the fact that there were no American gulags (Senator McCarran's prison camps were never used for interning 'subversives') makes the grotesqueries of the witch-hunt something trivial; or that preventing artists from working and then seeing to it that they cannot leave the country didn't mirror the political style of the enemy. Even if one concedes — as one must — that the leadership of the American Communist Party was utterly subservient to Stalin, it is still hard to see the purge of the 1950s as anything but a betrayal of the Constitution. It is difficult to understand what purpose was served by driving those who had signed petitions against the lynchings of negroes, or who had supported the Spanish Republic, out of their jobs in government or education. And it is all but impossible to find any principled reason for the purging of the reds, ex-reds and red-sympathisers from the film industry. For all that some movies of the 1940s and 1950s might have expressed implicitly subversive questions about big businessmen or sympathised with the little guy, even HUAC found it impossible to identify more than a handful of films with an 'un-American' or Communist message.

It wasn't until September 1984, after an exhaustive campaign by the historian John D Weaver, that the Motion Picture Academy finally gave Carl Foreman credit for the Oscar-winning screenplay of *The Bridge On the River Kwai*. By then he was already dead and his ashes on their way to England. I'm still trying to work out the irony. ❏

NOURI BOUZID

Mission unaccomplished

A lot has happened since 1988 when I filmed *Les Sabots en Or* (The Golden Shoes) that has made the film even more relevant today than it was at the time. It's about an Arab intellectual who finds himself trapped between a repressive government and Islamic fundamentalism; about a government that has allowed those who don't think to come to the fore in the process of repressing those who do. I wrote the screenplay in 1986/87, fearful of what would become of us. I kept telling myself there was no longer any place for intellectuals in our society. Arab intellectuals have failed in the task they set themselves: discouraged by repression and constant setbacks, under pressure from the rise of new forces and aware of their own failure and impotence, they've committed suicide.

In a sense, the film was prophetic, but, happily for us, the worst has not yet happened in Tunisia any more than in Morocco, both of which are relatively calm at the moment. To some extent, things have even moved back from the brink. In Algeria, on the other hand, things have reached crisis point. What's happening there should give pause for thought to anyone involved with ideas and social movements in the Mahgreb. Intellectuals are being assassinated. How has a country with such an elite reached such a catastrophic state of general ignorance and obscurantism? *Les Sabots en Or* more or less predicts such a situation but, contrary to the received version of events, the confrontation portrayed in the film is not between government and fundamentalists, but between the fundamentalists and the left. That's new and subversive: the confrontation between two rival schools of thought, progressive and obscurantist.

Tunisia has to some extent sorted its social problems — birth control, unemployment, housing, public transport, running water, food distribution. In Algeria difficulties are still acute. The move to arabisation was a serious setback: universities and high schools became the breeding ground of fundamentalists since those in charge of the arabisation programme were imported from Egypt, a country only too happy to be rid of its Muslim Brothers.

In Tunisia, intellectuals performed rather better than their counterparts in Algeria. Despite the paucity of their resources, they were more courageous in warning people of what was happening. This was certainly so as far as Perspectives [a left-wing organisation of which Bouzid was a member] was concerned. Let me cite another example: I've recently seen Merzak Allouache's film *Bab el Oued City.* It's an important film but it's too late: it should have been made 15 years ago. In Algeria they fastened on free expression when it was already too late; when the cancer had already taken hold of the body. And the price is human lives. Algerians are 'dying' from free expression.

We had the prescience to see what was going on and publicised it — in theatre, film and television — before it actually happened. As a result, we were accused of fomenting events when all we were doing was exposing the evil before it gained ground. We were simply doing our job: speaking out on forbidden subjects, breaking taboos. You don't find that in Algeria or Egypt.

The censors in Tunisia were shocked

LA MÉDIATHÈQUE DES TROIS MONDES

by the torture scenes in *Les Sabots en Or*, also by the love scene; by the
body in both guises: broken by torture and transported by joy. They
refused a certificate for the distribution of the film in Tunisia in its
original version. They wanted to cut it by 14 minutes, including the
crucial final scene between the two brothers, the intellectual and the
fundamentalist butcher. It's one of the strongest moments in the film and
I'd have made the whole thing for that one moment alone. It's a rare
moment in Arab cinema, one that challenges the whole Arab world
today. I refused to cut it and it remained banned for a year. Finally, after a
lot of negotiating, we reached a compromise: only three minutes would
be cut. In the end, and after more haggling, we got that down to 35
seconds: 20 from a torture scene; 15 from the lovemaking. And only for
screening in Tunisia; the negative remains intact.

I wanted to show the body in both situations: to make a film that
pushed out the limits of censorship, won some ground, enlarged the area
of free expression. Throughout the world, one of the most important
areas concerns portrayals of the body. As Arabs, this is nothing new for
us: we are familiar with it in our poetry. *One Thousand and One Nights*,
for instance, is as erotic as anything in the world. Even in the Quran
descriptions of the body are quite explicit. Now this territory has
become alien to us. While we can look at a foreign couple, we don't have
the right to look at Arab bodies making love. There's a danger that we
shall be reduced to voyeurs — constantly looking at others and never at
ourselves. The body in all its aspects should be available to drama. I
wanted to show my protagonist, the intellectual Youssouf Soltane, body
to body with a woman and rid myself of a complex.

The subject has always preoccupied me. In *L'Homme de Cendres* (Man
of Ashes) the body is wounded. In *Les Sabots en Or* I wanted to show that
the failed intellectual is burdened by his body; that just as under torture,
it bears the whole weight of the drama. In *Bezness* the body becomes the
object of perversion. Everything happens through the body; it's the only
thing left to sell. Moufida Tlatli's *Les Silences du Palais* (Silences of the
Palace) adopts the same approach: a young girl discovers her personal
drama at the same time as she discovers her body, with puberty and its
rules. The body is the key to one's identity. I'm all for a cinema of the
body.

While I want to test the limits of censorship, no film-maker actually
wants to be censored, even less his producer. We made the film as it was

in the approved screenplay. The trouble that followed demonstrates how much more powerful the image is than the written word. I certainly didn't court trouble, but I probably went too far in two different directions: I handed those who wanted to destroy the film — right-wing journalists for instance — the opportunity not to mention the torture scenes because they were all worked up over the love scene. I gave them the chance to jump onto the high moral ground.

Everything in the film is seen through Soltane's point of view. The audience sees only what he sees, what he hears from his past or present or what he imagines.

Here is a man who in the space of a night — the night of Ashura — searches in vain for somewhere to stay. He's been in prison for 10 years and is searching to put back together the pieces of his life. As he searches for those who were important in the past, he discovers the pieces have fragmented. The harder he tries to reconstruct them, the more he encounters things that shock and that scatter the fragments even further. In putting himself together he destroys. The film had to be structured in the same way: it gathers and then destroys with shocking images.

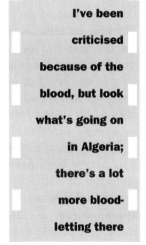

I've been criticised because of the blood, but look what's going on in Algeria; there's a lot more blood-letting there

Ashura is the night of tolerance, of forgiveness. It celebrates the salvation of the prophets: Abraham saved from fire, Noah from the flood, Jonah from the belly of the whale, Moses' crossing of the Red Sea, Mohammed's flight for his life from Mecca to Medina. But the time of salvation, the era of the prophets is over. Soltane, who saw himself as a prophet, will not be saved.

Ashura is also the night on which Hussein, the Prophet's grandson, was murdered. That's why there's a lot of blood in the film. I've been criticised because of the blood, but look what's going on in Algeria; there's a lot more blood-letting there. They don't just shoot people, they slit their throats, blood flows. People are terrorised by blood.

The general public in Tunisia found the film difficult to follow. I didn't set out to mystify but I wanted to take this approach as far as I could, to demonstrate there was only one specific way of telling the story.

Our own people are not used to such a flood of images or this type of structure. But, to my surprise, more people saw it than saw *L'Homme de Cendres*; 350,000 tickets sold.

What pleased me even more was that none of the groups portrayed were happy with the film, not the leftists, not the fundamentalists, even less the government. It's a film about politics but not the normal political film. It's a personal statement outside the standard political discourse. The method may not be to everyone's taste, some may find it shocking, but it works. As far as I'm concerned, it's the last word in the aesthetic portrayal of defeat, not in the military or political sense, but in that of the disintegration of an individual who has lost his sense of identity as he becomes brutally aware that he's no longer good for anything, that he's lost his place and his status. He's paid a high price for nothing, for hell.

It's not autobiography. There's a little of me in all the characters but it's not my life. I'm not dead, I've made a success of things. Maybe it's about what I've had to destroy in myself to become a success. Maybe it's even a film against myself.

I speak directly to my audiences. I accuse them but they don't feel it personally. I was a member of the extreme left but they see me simply as a subversive film-maker, once of the left. Initially, they are completely at sea; after about two years they accept my films. Cinema helps them understand themselves and the reasons for this burden of sorrow we carry around within us. Humiliation, defeat, so many shattered dreams have made us a people scarred by grief. I try to help them discover its causes through the emotions, not by moralising.

Les Sabots en Or is a 'post-ideological' film: indeed, it's against all ideology. It's only just been released but it was written nine years ago, well before the changes in the Soviet Union, yet it's very much in today's mood. My next film will look at the world of women from a woman's perspective; our women today, women who escape all the well known clichés. It will explore their situation and the difficulties they encounter in pursuit of their rights and dignity through an intimate look at two women, one of whom is divorced. The screenplay's already written and I hope I can start it soon. ❏

Reproduced courtesy of La Médiathèque des Trois Mondes
Translated by Judith Vidal-Hall

Steven Spielberg on the set of Schindler's List

Schindler's progress

January 1993 World Jewish Congress tries to prevent Spielberg shooting on location at Auschwitz. Vice-president Kalman Sultanik comments: '*Our concern is the preservation of the dignity of a place which is the largest Jewish burial ground in the world. We do not want it turned into a Hollywood back lot.*' Wiesenthal Centre backs Spielberg. Auschwitz State Museum director, Jerzy Wroblewski, urges the Polish government to support WJC.

February Spielberg agrees to shoot ome scenes outside the main ground and reconstruct the Plaszow labour camp in a quarry near Krakow. The WJC backs down.

June Anti-Semitic Poles in Krakow bars attack film cast.

December *Schindler's List* released in the United States.

February 1994 Film banned in **Indonesia**.

March Film banned in **Malaysia**. Film censor comments: '*The story reflects the privilege and virtues of a certain race only.*' A month later, Malaysian Film Censorship Appeal Committee overturns the ban but insists on seven cuts of violent or 'immoral' scenes. Distributors reject the cuts and the film remains unscreened. Film is not shown in **Dubai** where government information director says: '*We have no conflict with the Jews, only political problems with the Israelis. I don't believe this film can be shown until peace is fully established.*' Ban on film in **Philippines** for being too sexually explicit, overturned by President Ramos. Film banned in **Lebanon**.

April Jordan bans film. Information minister comments: '*At this stage, so soon after the Hebron massacre, emotions are running too high.*'

June In the USA, Khalid Abdul Muhamman (former spokesman for the Nation of Islam) comments: '*Schindler's List should be renamed* Swindler's List.*' **Egyptian** ban. Russian premiere of the film is postponed after Russian security discovers neo-Nazi group, The Werewolves, planning to assassinate Spielberg. It is finally screened in **September**.

Compiled by Anna Feldman

CONSTANTIN COSTA-GAVRAS

Politics and propaganda

Costa-Gavras is one of a select band who have made political cinema into big box-office and stayed independent on the way. Films like Z, Missing *and* Betrayed, *each of which tackled a hot political issue of their day, would, he thinks, have some difficulty getting through the US studio system today.* Z *(1969), a powerful indictment of the rule of the Colonels in Greece, and banned for many years in that country, is shown regularly today in memory and warning.* Missing *(1982), a big budget, big star movie, brought the horror of the disappeared in 1970s Latin America to a huge US audience.* Betrayed *(1989), a fiction built round disturbing factual material supplied by an unsuspecting FBI, was, say commentators, prophetic of the rise and rise of America's right-wing militias.*

At a time when mainstream political cinema is all but dead in the USA, the Greek film-maker, who is as much at home in Paris as in the studios of Paramount or Gaumont, draws the lines between propaganda, politics and the militant tendency; and points to the current political horizon

There are three quite different genres, often lumped together under the label 'committed' or 'propaganda' and usually identified with the left and against the establishment.

Film as propaganda par excellence stems from Stalin and Hitler. They created a whole industry simply to serve their specific ideology. A person like Eisenstein, for instance, began with a personal vision, he had personal and artistic freedom to express it. Later, he was forced by Stalin to serve the Communist vision. Leni Riefenstahl — such beautiful, dangerous films — was wholly an instrument of Hitler's system.

Militant cinema, such as we've seen in Latin America or France, can be about politics, religion, whatever, but it backs a particular idea and is frequently made with a one-way vision. The film-maker picks a side.

And then there are those people who have their own thoughts on society as a whole. They are independent of any party, ideology or movement and are judged only by the personal success of their film. I put myself in this group. Take *Minor Apocalypse* (1993), for instance. The people I portray there now run France: they own the press, politics, money. They are the bourgeois establishment. *Z* was accused of being propaganda when it was made. But it was financed independently to show a personal vision of what was happening in Greece at the time. Political films above all want to *show* — but there must be some meaning in what they show. You can take all sorts of artistic licence, but there must be facts — and witnesses. That is to say, testimony from one who is a witness to what is going on. Memory is crucial (to people and cultures): film must never be allowed to forget.

There's most certainly 'political' cinema in the USA today though it's something very different. *Forrest Gump* for instance. The most violent films, the banalisation of death, guns, evil, all picture the nature of US society. Tarantino may be a joke, but Oliver Stone's *Natural Born Killers* sucks in the audience, as does *Forrest Gump*. They create a political relationship with their audience. Film is the new 'opium of the people', TV sanitises, neutralises guns and evil. Take the TV treatment of the O J Simpson trial: it's OK to kill. Dole and his cronies are not really condemning violence, it's an election gimmick. The real violence is social evils like poverty, homelessness, unemployment and so on.

Interview by Sally Sampson and Judith Vidal-Hall

JUDITH VIDAL-HALL

ANDRZEJ WAJDA

Transformations in waiting

Man of Marble, 1977

In Dostoyevsky we read the following passage: 'Strange things began to happen in our town. One lieutenant took to lighting votive candles before the work of materialists; a woman began beating her children regularly, at the same time each day... We were free — but of what?'

For years, Polish film was free of an audience. Cinema-goers had no influence on our work because those in power didn't want people other than themselves to make critical judgements on them... I feel that freedom from an audience is something from which we still suffer.

Too many films are made without an interlocutor in mind. Something has happened to the ideology of cinema. The films we called 'the Polish school', 'the cinema of moral anxiety', and many others which didn't fall into either of these categories (like Zanussi's or Kieślowski's), were simply works emerging from a tradition fostered by the Polish nobility and inherited by the intelligentsia.

But just as the image of our leadership underwent a transformation with the aristocratic leader of the 1920s, Jozef Pilsudski, 'becoming' the worker, Lech Walesa, so the cultural tradition of the nobility must become the tradition of the people. Some films attempted to achieve this transition: Kazimierz Kutz tried to create a people's tradition in Polish cinema. He talked about it openly, and we accepted what he said.

Today, films are not seeking to counterpose the cultural tradition of the Polish gentry with a tradition that belongs to the people. The films we are seeing now are bourgeois films, petty bourgeois films aimed at the philistine, a viewer who wants only pleasure. And the director seeks to give that pleasure, whatever the cost, as though this were the last cinema-goer in the world. But is this the viewer we want? Must we really sacrifice so many films? Is the crisis of Polish cinematography merely economic?

Film has been atomised in its search for a viewer, and out of fear of that viewer. There is an absence of shared vision, of evaluation; and I believe that now, more than ever, we need to evaluate. Polish film is threatened most of all by a lack of orientation among film-makers who often don't seem to be aware of where and when they are living. We are dealing with a crisis in the art of the cinema, a crisis in our innermost way of thinking. I say this to myself as well, because if I knew what kind of film to make, I'd have made it by now. I wouldn't be waiting...

It is hard to make films for today and hard to break out of the crisis. But there is no other way.

© *Edited extracts from 'Freedom from what?', speech given at Gdynia Film Festival, September 1991. Published in Polish in* Kino (Cinema) 1/1992
Translated by Irena Maryniak

KRZYSZTOF KIEŚLOWSKI

Quality cuts

Essentially, censorship lay in ourselves — the writers, directors and dramatists. That was where we sensed it most. And in the officials who were professionally engaged in 'minding' us, disrupting our work and, at times, helping us too. They weren't exclusively concerned with disruption. It wasn't like that. There were those who wanted to help, and did. Paradoxically, people engaged in cultural censorship have an interest in maintaining a culture of quality because their own role depends on its existence. Without culture, censorship loses its *raison d'être*.

Of course, there was a time when I was fearful. 'Fear' is such a mild word. I never felt that cinema was the most important part of my life. I still don't. But it's my profession, so the anxiety is there — that I won't be able to make the next film, that it will be ill-received or released down a blind alley. There was a time when we feared to expose ourselves and stick out our necks, even as we constantly did so. We tried to reach out to the limit, to find the sharp end of the blade. We played games with censorship, while fearing at the same time that we'd lose and be unable to make something later on.

I once did a film for television called *Spokoj* (Calm) of which I was very fond, and still am, even though I changed it as a result of intervention from the censor. State television had a particularly cunning — almost diabolical — figure of a vice-chairman at the time. He summoned me to see him, so I went. It was quite clear what he wanted. I knew that he intended to cut. He was very charming, very intelligent and precise. He liked the film and spoke about it briefly, and I saw that he had understood everything, even the most subtle, hidden levels of human emotion. But I realised that he hadn't called me in to flatter me. He wanted to cut. It was the scene where the hero, a former prisoner (played beautifully by Jurek Stuhr) meets his fellow prison inmates on a building site. They are working there and so is he, as a free man.

The vice-chairman said that the scene had to be cut because an international convention makes it illegal for prisoners to work on a building site. 'OK,' I said, 'but take a look through that window.' (I had noted a little scene outside the television building as I was going in.)

'Take a look at the tramlines,' I said, 'and tell me what you see.'

He walked up to the window, because he was polite, and said: 'I can see people at work.'

'Take a closer look,' I said.

'Prisoners,' he said.

'So it's not true that prisoners don't work outside in the street. You can see them.'

'Which is the very reason why the scene must go. In Poland prisoners are not permitted to work in public places: international law forbids it.'

'But they do, you can see them through the window.'

'Of course I can. That's why you've got to cut the scene.'

So, of course, I did. I cut a great deal from my films — when I thought that the cuts wouldn't spoil the essence of the film. In some cases I refused and the films weren't shown. *Spokoj* was never shown in any case.

In the 1970s, the era of the 'cinema of moral anxiety' — a phrase I detest — film-makers and viewers communicated over the heads of the censors. We were forced to find dramatic and intellectual resolutions which we thought viewers would understand and the censors wouldn't.

And it turned out that this world shown in microcosm was being seen by viewers as a generalised picture of life in Poland. We functioned in this way because we felt that it was our task to depict the world, the *real* world which wasn't being shown on the screen at that time — because the censors, the Party, the government, the echelons of power (call them what you will) didn't want it, because the world wasn't what it should be. Why did they devise censorship? To show a world which doesn't exist, an ideal world, or what they envisaged as the ideal world. And we wanted to depict the world as it was.

© *Edited excerpts from 'Tren na smiere cenzora' (Lament on the death of a censor), published in* Rezyser, *co-published with* Kino II/*1992*
Translated by Irena Maryniak

NADEZHDA POKORNAYA

Festivals, films and fireworks

Just before my September trip to Moscow I came across a photograph of MosFilm studios in *Le Monde* and it frightened me. The once renowned studios resembled the city of Stalingrad after the last bombing attack of World War II. Yet what I saw when I got there was nothing of the kind. MosFilm had been transformed from a film studio into a complex consisting of 10 independent studios. Of course instead of producing 150 films a year as they did in the wasteful days of hard-core socialism, MosFilm today makes at most 30, a figure, like everything else these days, dictated by the free market: none of the former republics of the USSR, now independent states, can any longer be forced to purchase Russian films.

Like the city of Moscow itself, MosFilm looks something between a heap of debris and a construction site — but only at a first glance. Those who visit Moscow regularly can see that practically everything is in a ferment of reorganisation; its hardly surprising that at this stage nobody can guess what the prospects are for any future enterprise.

A couple of months ago the multi-million dollar XIX Film Festival resounded throughout Moscow. The money was allocated by prime minister Viktor Chernomyrdin from the state budget — money that should have been used on new films. Fireworks danced in the Moscow sky in honour of the festival while Russian film-makers looked on and counted: there goes my pre-production, and there's the stock and the cutting equipment... Guests from the West were lavishly welcomed with caviar and champagne, taken on boat cruises. Their entertainment programme was exceptional, even including a prison 'reception': the chairman of the festival, Richard Gere, spent one night in Nizhny Novgorod remand centre for purchasing 25 kilos of poachers' caviar. Subsequently his agent apologised for this incident from the stage, assuring the audience that Mr Gere was not a speculator. Everybody applauded hysterically as a token of sympathy. The critics who related this to me couldn't conceal their sarcasm; they are gloomy about the situation in the film industry. 'There used to be slogans all around us saying 'THE ARTS BELONG TO THE PEOPLE!' Now it's clear without any slogans that our diseased arts belong to the diseased people...'

Russian cinemas are overloaded with western thrillers and erotic films. Russian films are not being advertised or purchased by distributors for mass demonstration. A recent sociological poll suggests that the culture of cinema-going can never be revived. To boost profits, managers of uncomfortable and untidy cinemas are compelled to rent their space out for discos and as sale rooms for western cars. There is a lot to be said about the problems of distribution, but there is little doubt that for those who control it, the 'blockade' of Russian films on the home market is a profitable business. On the other hand, take Vladimir Menshov's film *Shyrli-Myrli*. Financed by MosFilm and RosKomKino, it cost US$7 million, enough for the average budget of six films. The film was particularly well advertised and distributed and became more popular than all the American thrillers.

The state continues to sponsor its favourite directors. Thus *To love à la Russe* [director Eugeny Matueev] was made exclusively on the funds provided by the Ministry of Finance. Meanwhile at the XIX Film Festival the Russian minister of cinematography made an appeal to the Russian people to contribute money for the sequel to this blockbuster. 'Make the first "people's" film!' On which my friend Olga Henkina, a critic, commented: 'I pity those who have not yet seen *To love à la Russe*. It's now my favourite film. I used to think the summits of idiocy were conquered, but I was wrong. Marvellous film! There's never been better quality pornography. If the director films a bare bottom, then he does it in such a way that nobody would want to look at any other. How skilfully the protagonist tries to get under his female co-star's skirt. After seeing that you'd never want sex again...'

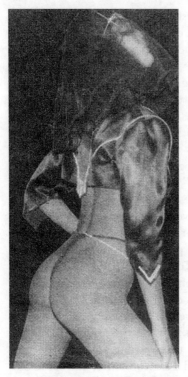

Ilyinskaya's The Masked Sinner

In the course of my visit — just eight days — I watched the rapid politicisation of film-makers who appeared on television and radio. Many eminent directors and actors have hastily joined the ranks of various parties and political blocs on the eve of the elections, as if in response to a war-cry: 'The place of an artiste is in the State Council!' Politicians have always exploited artistes; some may really believe culture will save the world, others simply get what they can out of the famous names.

In the last two years the subject-matter of films has changed. The age of pornography and dark, heavy films is coming to an end and the latest fashion is Russian melodrama. According to Paola Volkova, a tutor at the Higher Screenwriters/Directors School, 'The pendulum of art is swinging in the other direction. It had become too much of a formula and the reaction has now set in.'

Volkova is right. For five years we have been learning all sorts of filth about ourselves; this filth was transferred to the screen and, frequently, vice versa. The Frankenstein monster stepped from free, post-Soviet Russian cinema into life. At first it frightened everybody a good deal, then it started to get on people's nerves like an obtrusive fly. Now people are starting to forget about it. Violent feature films have lost their appeal for film-makers as well as their audiences. Only Frankenstein's half-dressed bride still appears now and then in newly fashionable erotic melodramas. But for some reason she covers her face, as, for example, in Svetlana Ilyinskaya's *The Masked Sinner*, co-written with US and German screenwriters. The film is about a very beautiful actress disfigured in a car crash. Since she cannot afford plastic surgery, she takes a job in a sex show, hiding her face under a veil. Her objective is not only to earn some dosh, but to prove the power of her talent and recover her face, evidently by revealing her backside. Advertising insists this 'gripping' film is potentially a winner with distributors.

To be fair I should say that there are other films and their number is increasing. Many directors have turned to classics: Roman Balayan — Turgenev's *First Love*. Vladimir Dostal — Sologub's *Small Devil*. A Sakharov — Pushkin's *A Young Peasant Lady;* and several directors are indebted to Chekhov. Under dictatorship escapist cinema was made to avoid the nausea of social realism. Nowadays, directors are tired of quasi-democracy. Besides, there's no need to beg money from sponsors when they can get state funds for Pushkin.

In the course of the last two years, films on the new Russians, by the new Russians, and frequently financed by the new, right-wing bourgeoisie, have begun to appear on the Russian market. They are about people — or to be more precise, about certain types — who encapsulate the essence of our time. For example, Denis Evstigneev's *Limita* and Valery Todorovsky's 1995 *Moscow Suburban Nights*. They have divided the critics, so I went and asked Todorovsky about the effect of the abolition of state censorship on films and about the problems directors were having to cope with now.

At first we saw freedom as a blessing. But now this freedom has turned into problems — a fear of freedom has emerged, problems of choosing subject, genre, money, of film financing. Directors have divided into two groups: those capable of surviving competition and those who were crushed by it. The viewers have their freedom — now they choose what they want to see. Distributors deal only with what is profitable. All this threatened the Russian film industry with disintegration. But it has recovered. A new entity has appeared on the Russian market — producers. They brought the rules of survival in the free market. There are victims, but some have gained — me, for example. I have accepted the need to find financing for new films, on top of being just a creator; it's part of the job, not a tragedy. Abolition of state censorship has brought freedom of travel and we started going to western countries, to the festivals; wherever I went I made new friends in the film industry. But the free market is traumatic. Many one-time successful directors had to step aside — such stars of the 1970s cinema as Eldar Ryzanov, Vitaly Melnikov, Igor Maslennikov, Semyon Aranovich. On the other hand, Mikhalkov continues working and very successfully.

The Oscar for his *Burnt by the Sun* is a victory after all. The current situation is especially hard on the generation whom so far nobody knows. A beginner has to make a talented half-penny film so that he is noticed and considered worth financing. To survive, a director has to make one film a year. A cameraman costs up to US$20,000, rent of equipment US$5-6,000. *Love*, which I made in 1992, cost 900,000 roubles, while *Moscow Suburban Nights* in 1994 cost US$ 5,000,000 and was financed by the French Film Aid Institute. I consider myself very lucky professionally. I have managed to survive in this new financial war.

In an interview with the monthly *Kino-glaz* (Cinema Eye) this year, director Sergei Solovyev, chairman of the Union of Film-makers of Russia, spoke about this new world.

'With the disintegration of the USSR the social system, which guaranteed work to everyone who had a degree, has disintegrated as well. In the last couple of years production of films has substantially reduced, the threat of unemployment has reared its head, professional criteria were lost — those who managed to find the money would make the films. At present we have surmounted the crisis of the industry, largely owing to the fact that the Union of Film-makers, has been preserved. Today Russia produces about 100 feature films per year, 90 of them financed by the state (with funds provided by sponsors). Out of those 100, two to three are very good, 10 decent. While in the past popular production was based on the taste of Party bosses, now it caters for the most common, vulgar taste of an average viewer. We don't have censorship as we did in the past and it's unclear what's worse: the ugliness in our films exceeds anything on the world screen. The tastes of those with the money become the criteria for evaluating a film. Our cinematography has never been the financial phenomenon it is in Hollywood; it has always been guided by cultural values. Andrei Tarkovsky said film is the highest form of poetry. The empire is a thing of the past and politically we are deeply divided now. Cinema guided by true art should unite us.' ❏

Mikhalkov and Nadia in Burnt by the Sun, *1995*

NIKITA MIKHALKOV

The sun also rises

'Today, it's very important to bear witness, because the children don't understand. For example, Nadia, my eight-year-old daughter, doesn't understand the word "Soviet"... It's not a question of boasting about the charm of the Soviet Union. I believe that the sun will rise whatever the regime, but one must be on one's guard, ready for a different sun to rise... It's not a question of choosing the moments in our history which seem to us the best. We must recognise that there were moments of heroism, but also moments of shame, injustice, indignity, humiliation. We must understand clearly that we are all responsible, and that there are some among us who must carry the burden of this responsibility...'

1896: No news footage from Imperial Russia

Francis Doublier initiated film production in Russia on 14 May 1896 when he shot the coronation of Tsar Nicholas II. Two days later he was present at a feudal ceremony at which the new Tsar was presented to his subjects. Doublier and his assistant, Moisson, set up their camera on the roof of an unfinished building near the Tsar's stand. Doublier recalled what happened next:

'We arrived about eight o'clock in the morning because the ceremony was due to take most of the day, and the Tsar was to arrive early. When I saw some of the souvenirs being handed out ahead of time, I got down and pushed through the very dense crowd to the booths, about 150 feet away. On the way back, the crowd began to push, impatient with the delay and by the time I got within 25 feet of our camera, I heard shrieks behind me and panic spread through the people. I climbed onto a neighbour's shoulders and struggled across the top of the frightened mass. That 25 feet seemed like 25 miles, with the crowd underneath clutching desperately at my feet and biting my legs. When I finally reached the roof again, we were so nervous that we were neither able to guess the enormity of the tragedy nor to turn the camera crank. The light boarding over two large cisterns had given way, and into these and into the ditches near the booths hundreds had fallen, and in the panic thousands more had fallen and been trampled to death. When we came to our senses we began to film the horrible scene. We had brought only five or six of the 60-foot rolls, and we used up three of these on the shrieking, milling, dying mass around the Tsar's canopy where we had expected to film a very different scene. I saw the police charging the crowd in an effort to stop the tidal wave of human beings. We were completely surrounded and it was only two hours later that we were able to think about leaving the place strewn with mangled bodies. Before we could get away the police spotted us, and added us to the bands of arrested correspondents and witnesses. All our equipment was confiscated and we never saw our precious camera again. Because of the camera we were particularly suspect, and we were questioned and detained until the evening, when the Consul vouched for us.'

© *Excerpted from Jay Leyda,* Kino: A History of Russian and Soviet Film; *Allen & Unwin (1960)*

JIŘÍ MENZEL

The art of laughter and survival

With his latest film, *The Life and Extraordinary Adventures of Private Ivan Chonkin*, Czech director Jiří Menzel is back in Schweik country: the little man against the power of the world's biggest army. But with more warmth and humour than the Good Soldier ever encountered. That, says Menzel, 'is because it's by a Russian', as a result of which, it nearly didn't get made at all. Post-Soviet film-goers might have been ready for Ivan, the generals of the Red Army were not.

Russian satirist Vladimir Voinovich's novel from which the film was made has an all too familiar history. It made its appearance in 1968 but circulated only in *samizdat* until, by the same route as Solzhenitsyn and Pasternak — the Paris YMCA — it made its way to the West and was published in 1989 in Russian and English to extravagant critical acclaim. 'A new Gogol come among us', declared the *New York Times;* 'a Soviet Catch 22'. It was praised for its 'liberating power of laughter' but the Soviet authorities were not amused and the novelist found himself minus passport and nationality teaching in Munich. In 1990, Chonkin made his first legitimate appearance in the Russian literary journal *Yunost*; the satirical tale was labelled 'blasphemous', and Voinovich accused of being a 'traitor' and 'slanderer' by the generals it lampooned.

So Chonkin came home with Menzel and was filmed in the Czech Republic, with Russian actors and in its original language: the 'little man' with the big soul pitted against the 'masked' guys of state and bureaucracy are Menzel's stock in trade. His Oscar-winning *Closely Observed Trains* of 1966 established the wry humour and human compassion that became his hallmark. His next film, *Larks on a String*, unfinished when the Soviet tanks burst on Prague in 1968, moves into the hinterland of the absurd where, as in fellow Czech Ivan Klíma's *Love and Garbage*, written almost 20 years later, philosophical work gangs,

diverted thence from loftier climes for the good of their ideological
health, labour over the city's refuse or, in Menzel's case, displace the
state's rusting surplus production from one pile of scrap to another of
junk. In one sublime episode, the latest arrival of redundant metal — a
load of assorted typewriters — is passed unremarked and with tender care
from skip to crusher. While Menzel never claims to be a dissident, he was
never quite of the 'official line' and his films, at least, were seen as
profoundly subversive. It took the recalcitrant, Party-defying heroes of
Larks 22 years to reach the public for whom they had been intended.

Menzel's humour is stoic and timeless, a manner of surviving. For
seven years after *Larks* he was prevented from directing and remained
officially a 'non-person'. Unlike so many of his countrymen and women,
and despite invitations to work abroad, he stayed on, continuing to
entertain and instruct the little people who had nowhere else to go.
Today, his films are seen throughout the Republic.

'It's perfectly natural to stay on in your own place: I had this film to
finish, I'm lazy — a frequent accusation — not very ambitious and I
had these elderly parents. [His father was a journalist, imprisoned by the
Nazis and later by the Communists for refusing to join the Party.] Maybe
I just lacked the courage. I'm against emigration for purely economic
reasons; and if all the enemies of the system get out, it makes it so much
easier for the regime.

'Milos [Forman] had to go. He made different, very good movies out
there he couldn't have made if he'd stayed. After *The Firemen's Ball,* they
were after him. Like Chagall, if he hadn't gone — and here a graphic
slice with the forefinger across the throat — they might have killed him.
In any case, not every film-maker can go to Hollywood: there have to be
some left to make movies in other countries for people there.

'But basically, I didn't think the whole business would last so long: a
few months maybe, not 22 years.

'People — the authorities — were very angry after *Larks on a String*
was finally shown. Regimes are afraid of humour because it's more direct,
clearer to the audience. Small nations and societies survive through
humour. Sometimes it's all they have: look at Jewish humour. When I
was a small boy, my mother used to scold me with humour, not anger.
Irony is more painful; criticism by humour cuts straight into the
conscience, wakes it up. It's a much better way of communicating

JIRI MENZEL'S
COMEDY

THE LIFE AND EXTRAORDINARY
ADVENTURES OF PRIVATE IVAN
CHONKIN

PORTOBELLO PICTURES

important things. The same things said in earnest make a man think you're the enemy and he closes his ears to anything else. Humour, satire doesn't appear to threaten or destroy; it demolishes from within. It's the ultimate subversion.

'The fact that the film [*Chonkin*] happens in wartime — like *Closely*

Observed Trains it takes place during World War II — is purely accidental. I don't like war and there is nothing heroic about it. Except for the "little people". They don't wear a mask like the big guys who pretend to be something else and cease to be private people. Big does not equal heroic. Little people, the people of my films, are unconscious heroes; their everyday life makes them heroic but they don't see it.

'We Czechs are little and unheroic, not like the Poles. We wouldn't charge out on horseback against tanks. We've always been occupied by the enemy — Austrians, Germans, Russians. We've learned to live with the tanks: we make contracts with the enemy, not conflict. Now we're not only free, we have no enemies! Europe is calm, the economy's doing well, we inherited few debts and we have Mr Klaus [as prime minister]. Everybody likes him because, like them, he may not be very clever but he does know what he's doing. He's doing well in the polls: 50 per cent say they like him; 90 per cent say they can't think of a replacement.

'What are we doing with this freedom? Unlike Poles who are all petit aristocrats, Czechs are all petit bourgeois. In the 1950s and 1960s work was a dirty word and workmen were no longer proud of what they made. I thought people would never learn to work honestly again. But I was wrong: the petit bourgeois sense has returned in a positive way. I hear the Czech language when I go abroad. People are travelling; they're hungry to see the world now they have the chance. And they're not beggars: they have their own money and can stay in decent hotels. The little man has found his self-confidence.

'Intellectuals, creative people? That's more difficult. There are no limits and therefore no boundaries within which to create. That boundary between us and the West makes us hunger for what is on the other side. We want to be more Catholic than the Pope. We consume the garbage because it's available now. There's also a tendency to make art for art's sake. I need a reason for what I do. Before it was easy. It's not enough just to want to be rich and famous. It's difficult to formulate a motive. The New Wave was created by the constraints of Communism; now we can say anything — and there's nothing to say.'

The Life and Extraordinary Adventures of Private Ivan Chonkin was released in the UK in late October to disappointing reviews. Maybe Menzel's right: art needs an enemy. ❏

Interview by Judith Vidal-Hall

PETER HAMES

Permanent subversion

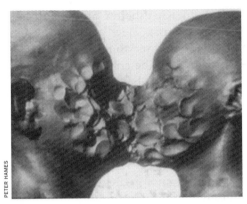

PETER HAMES

Dimensions of Dialogue, 1982

All animators, it has been said, are surrealists. Jan Švankmajer, a Czech animator as well as a practising surrealist, began work on his first film in 1958. In the last 10 years he has become an international name, attracting something of a cult following with feature films such as *Alice* (1987) and *Faust* (1994).

The Czech tradition of animation is well known. In the 1950s, when fiction films conformed to the worst kinds of Stalinist orthodoxy, directors such as Jiří Trnka and Karel Zeman established a world reputation and challenged Disney conventions. Visual experiment survived in this permitted framework when avant-garde and surrealist work was officially proscribed. Similarly, during the 20-year repression that followed the Soviet invasion of 1968, Švankmajer practised a unique brand of subversion when feature films were often confined to a naive humanism.

If the animation ghetto provided a space in which Švankmajer could work, five of his films were nonetheless banned and he was unable to work at all between 1973-1980. *Dimensions of Dialogue* (1982) was shown to the ideology commission of the Communist Party as an example of what had to be avoided. His work did not really reach domestic audiences until after his international success in the late 1980s.

Many of his films can be viewed politically. *The Flat* (1968) features a man locked in a room from which he cannot escape while *The Garden* (1968) is set in a house surrounded by a human fence. The hero of *The Pendulum, the Pit and Hope* (1983) escapes from an underground torture chamber to confront a caped figure who blocks his escape in the name of 'brotherhood'. In one of the sections of *Dimensions of Dialogue*, the dialectic of mutually devouring heads gives way to a sequence of identical production-line models.

In *The Death of Stalinism in Bohemia* (1990), which he describes as a work of agitprop, he deals directly with the post-war history of Czechoslovakia. As Stalin gives way to Khrushchev and Brezhnev, Gottwald and Novotný to Dubček and Husák, new orthodoxies and compromises emerge. At the end of the film, everything — jugs, petrol cans, a bust of Stalin, old tyres — is painted in the colours of the Czech flag. Hands rummage in the entrails of Stalin's head. A baby cries. A question mark hangs over the new democracy.

Like fellow surrealist, Luis Buñuel, Švankmajer shares a black view of human relations. From his first film as a director, *The Last Trick of Mr Schwarzwald and Mr Edgar* (1964), through *Punch and Judy/The Coffin House* (1966) to *Dimensions of Dialogue* and *Food* (1992), he often presents a destructive interplay in which opposing figures dismember and devour each other. In *Dimensions of Dialogue,* love between man and woman moves from romance to passion and mutual destruction. In *Food*, having been deprived of a meal, two diners eat everything in sight, including forks, clothes, and chairs. At the end of the sequence, one of them is poised to eat his fellow. 'Destruction in my films', argues Švankmajer, 'has ideological and philosophical roots.' A necessary corrective, perhaps, to a world in which slogans of socialism and peace cloaked a police state and where notions of freedom and democracy interact with new forms of colonialism.

Much of the unique power of his films, a sense of near physical impact, comes from the senses of touch and texture, combined with a special approach to the life of objects. 'I prefer the kind of objects which...have some kind of inner life... I am becoming more aware of the fact that, to revive the general impoverishment of sensibility in our civilisation, the sense of touch may play an important part.'

Švankmajer works very much in the surrealist tradition of permanent revolution. Above all, he stresses, surrealism is not art. 'Surrealism is a

Faust, *1994: surreal weapon against spiritual decay*

journey into the soul, like alchemy and psychoanalysis.' Its central aim remains that of changing the world (Marx) and changing life (Rimbaud). 'To continue to hold these beliefs in Czechoslovakia means to risk denunciation for "crypto-Communism" — regardless of the fact that surrealism opposed Communist practices during the whole period of Stalinist totality.' Since the lyrical surrealism of the 1930s, the world has seen World War II, Stalinism, ecological catastrophe and the triumph of consumer ideology — the products of what Vratislav Effenberger, post-war leader of the Czech surrealists and much admired by Švankmajer, refers to as 'decadent rationality'. 'More adequate weapons against this spiritual decay', argues Švankmajer, 'are sarcasm, cynicism, imagination and mystification.'

Capitalism has given Švankmajer the opportunity to realise long-cherished projects: *Faust* was first written in the early 1980s, *Food* in the early 1970s; his imagery has been recycled in numerous television adverts, and he has worked for MTV and directed a music video for the punk-rock group The Stranglers (*Another Kind of Love*). Consistently oppositional, Švankmajer's films combine both an aesthetic and intellectual challenge. His new film, *Conspirators of Pleasure*, promises a controversial mix of magic and erotic — like *Faust*, a reminder that the end of one political system has not removed his essential subject matter. ❏

JEAN VIGO

The terrible Luis Buñuel

Un Chien Andalou, though primarily a subjective drama fashioned into a poem, is none the less, in my opinion, a film of social consciousness.

Un Chien Andalou is a masterwork from every aspect: its certainty of direction, its brilliance of lighting, its perfect amalgam of visual and ideological associations, its sustained dream-like logic, its admirable confrontation between the subconscious and the rational.

Considered in terms of social consciousness, *Un Chien Andalou* is both precise and courageous.

Incidentally I would like to make the point that it belongs to an extremely rare class of film.

I have met M Louis Buñuel [sic] only once and then only for ten minutes, and our meeting in no way touched upon *Un Chien Andalou*. This enables me to discuss it with much greater liberty. Obviously my comments are entirely personal. Possibly I will get near the truth, without doubt I will commit some howlers.

In order to understand the significance of the film's title it is essential to remember that M Buñuel is Spanish.

An Andalusian dog howls — who then is dead?

Our cowardice, which leads us to accept so many of the horrors that we, as a species, commit, is dearly put to the test when we flinch from the screen image of a woman's eye sliced in half by a razor. Is it more dreadful than the spectacle of a cloud veiling a full moon?

Such is the prologue: it leaves us with no alternative but to admit that we will be committed, that in this film we will have to view with something more than the everyday eye.

Throughout the film we are held in the same grip.

From the first sequence we discern, beneath the image of an overgrown child riding up the street without touching the handlebars, hands on his thighs, covered with white frills like so many wings, we discern, I repeat, our truth which turns to cowardice in contact with the world which we accept, (one gets the world one deserves), this world of

MOMA STILLS ARCHIVE

Luis Buñuel stars in Un Chien Andalou, *1929*

inflated prejudices, of betrayals of one's inner self, of pathetically romanticised regrets.

M Buñuel is a fine marksman who disdains the stab in the back.

A kick in the back to macabre ceremonies, to those last rites for a being no longer there, who has become no more than a dust-filled hollow down the centre of the bed.

A kick in the pants to those who have sullied love by resorting to rape.

To cultivate a

socially aware

cinema is to

ensure a cinema

which deals with

subjects which

provoke interest,

of subjects whicl

cut ice...

A kick in the pants to sadism, of which buffoonery is its most disguised form.

And let us pluck a little at the reins of morality with which we harness ourselves.

Let's see a bit of what is at the end.

A cork, here is a weighty argument.

A melon — the disinherited middle classes.

Two priests — alas for Christ!

Two grand pianos, stuffed with corpses and excrement — our pathetic sentimentality.

Finally, the donkey in close-up. We were expecting it.

M Buñuel is terrible.

Shame on those who kill in youth what they themselves would have become, who seek, in the forests and along the beaches, where the sea casts up our memories and regrets the dried-up projection of their first blossoming.

Cave canem...

All this written in an attempt to avoid too arid an analysis, image by image, in any case impossible in a good film whose savage poetry exacts respect — and with the sole aim of creating the desire to see or see again *Un Chien Andalou*. To cultivate a socially aware cinema is to ensure a cinema which deals with subjects which provoke interest, of subjects which cut ice...

© *Jean Vigo in* Vers un Cinéma Social, *1930 Reprinted from* Un Chien Andalou *by Luis Buñuel and Salvador Dali, (Faber and Faber, 1994)*

Julian Barnes
Lionel Blue
Joseph Brodsky
A S Byatt
Beatrix Campbell
Noam Chomsky
Alan Clark
Emma Donoghue
Ariel Dorfman
Ronald Dworkin
Umberto Eco
James Fenton
Paul Foot
Zufar Gareev
Timothy Garton Ash
Martha Gellhorn
Nadine Gordimer
Gunter Grass
Vaclav Havel
Christopher Hitchens
Ryszard Kapuscinski
Yasar Kemal
Helena Kennedy
Ivan Klima
Doris Lessing
Mario Vargas Llosa
Naguib Mahfouz
Alberto Manguel
Arthur Miller
Caroline Moorehead
Aryeh Neier
Harold Pinter
Salman Rushdie
Edward Said
Posy Simmonds
John Simpson
Alexander Solzhenitsyn
Wole Soyinka
Stephen Spender
Tatyana Tolstaya
Alex de Waal
Edmund White
Vladimir Zhirinovsky

'INDEX *has bylines that Vanity Fair would kill for. Would that bylines were the only things about* INDEX *people were willing to kill for.*'

—Boston Globe

United Kingdom & Overseas (excluding USA & Canada)

	UK:	Overseas:	Students: £25
1 year—6 issues	£32	£38	
2 years—12 issues	£59	£70	
3 years—18 issues	£85	£105	

Name

Address

Postcode

£ _____ total.

❑ Cheque (£) ❑ Visa/Mastercard ❑ Am Ex ❑ Diners Club

Card No.

Expiry   Signature   B5A6

❑ I would also like to send **INDEX** to a reader in the developing world—just £22. These sponsored subscriptions promote free speech around the world for only the cost of printing and postage.

Return to: INDEX, Freepost, 33 Islington High Street, London N1 9BR
Telephone: 0171 278 2313   **Facsimile:** 0171 278 1878

United States and Canada

	US$:	Students: $35
1 year—6 issues	$48	
2 years—12 issues	$90	
3 years—18 issues	$136	

Name

Address

Postcode

$ _____ total.

❑ Cheque (US$) ❑ Visa/Mastercard ❑ Am Ex ❑ Diners Club

Card No.

Expiry   Signature   B5B6

❑ I would also like to send **INDEX** to a reader in the developing world—just $33. These sponsored subscriptions promote free speech around the world for only the cost of printing and postage.

INDEX ON CENSORSHIP

33 Islington High Street, London N1 9LH England   Facsimile: 0171 278 2313

BUSINESS REPLY SERVICE
Licence No. LON 6323

INDEX ON CENSORSHIP
33 Islington High Street
London N1 9BR
United Kingdom

NO POSTAGE
NECESSARY
IF MAILED
IN THE
UNITED STATES

BUSINESS REPLY MAIL
FIRST CLASS PERMIT NO.7796 NEW YORK, NY

Postage will be paid by addressee.

INDEX ON CENSORSHIP
215 Park Avenue South
11th Floor
New York, NY 10211-0997

MILOS FORMAN

It's good out in the jungle

'Everything that is noble, and that has remained in art and literature since ancient times and that is also significant for strong contemporary works of art, has always concerned itself with injuries and injustices against the individual. That is because we always perceive the work of art as individuals. There, at the bottom of all those great works of art, are the injustices which no social order will eliminate.'

High sounding sentiments, pompous even, from a man who professes to have no time for the moral abstraction or heroic ideal. Neither in life nor in art. Maybe it's just a case of the word made redundant: failing to achieve what the image has already done so many times and so much more succinctly.

In the flesh, as in his films, Milos Forman presents a different image. Urbane, quiet, a European of the enlightenment despite almost 30 years in the USA; huge energy contained behind thick, heavily-framed lenses, somehow larger than life in the genteel pastiche rococo of one of Paris's more discreet hotels favoured by those of a publicity-hungry business who seek privacy rather than the paparazzi.

He engages with ideas, coiling back on an earlier thought to develop an idea in perpetual motion, talking the while of such things as the perils of freedom or dictatorship, the survival of small nations, the 'absurdity' of censorship, the over-rated power and passing pleasure of the movies, the ambivalent joys of the Internet — just another means of distribution — and the rights of individuals, life, art and what passes for both, not as one who panders to these particular concerns out of courtesy, but with passion informed by experience. His next film, *People versus Larry Flint*, due at the end of 1996, confronts free expression head on. Almost; it's more of an out-flanking approach.

'Larry Flint was the editor of *Hustler*, the lowest form of bad taste pornography. But we owe him a lot. The magazine was sued by the right-wing moral crusader Jerry Falwell in the 1980s and Flint ultimately censored by a bullet that paralysed him and left him in constant pain. He became a junkie, his wife took an overdose. He had his spinal cord severed; there was no pain, but no control over bodily functions either. He went cold turkey, made a million dollars and took his case to the supreme court. He got the most important judgement ever for free expression in America.'

There's the paradox again: noble victories in a lousy cause. Not so lousy: 'The first thing the Nazis and Communists attacked were sex, deviation, pornography. Prostitution's older than censorship, you'll never beat it, but it was an excuse to inflict fear and impose power; everything else followed. Today it's the right-wing militias who're screaming loudest for a free press. Freedom *is* indivisible, even when it brings to power those who will curtail it for others. Excesses are the price we pay to protect it for all. I remember the films of Leni Riefenstahl. They were beautiful. I loved them. I don't think they touched my feelings, but they probably left an impression at the time. If anti-Nazi stuff had also been allowed, rival propagandas could have fought it out.'

Born in small-town Czechoslovakia in 1932, Forman has been a participant, willing or not, in most of the 'big ideas of our time': Nazism carried off both parents to die in concentration camps when he was a child; Communism dominated and then curtailed his working years in Czechoslovakia; Hollywood beckoned and he was plunged into the delights and despairs of market capitalism. Having sampled all, the realist has time for none. There is a paradox — a favourite word that peppers his conversation and provides a unifying motive in works as different as *One Flew Over the Cuckoo's Nest*, *Amadeus* or *The Firemen's Ball* — at the heart of freedom as in the mind of the dictator. Human nature is ambiguous; the individual will always be at odds with any system; outsiders that society can neither comprehend nor contain will be the victims of even the most benign social order. Forman films have no larger than life heroes or anti-heroes as do US films and fables: the genius Mozart is neither the appealing child prodigy nor the uniform high-tone man; the fixed grimace of the criminally insane — perhaps? — McMurphy who turns the well-meaning establishment on its head, is no conventional liberator of men. His approach to the ambiguities and complexities of man and systems is that of a pessimistic humanist: 'The individual will never win these battles; the people in the system have a right to their lives too.' But an optimist in the long-term evolution of systems and the survival of the spirit that opposes their instinct to control. His tools are a compassionate humour, tragi-comic irony that looks beneath the surface and finds things not quite as conventional wisdom would have us believe. Genius is rejected by mediocrity — all systems are mediocre — but the high priest of the mediocre, Salieri, blesses his tribe as he passes through the ranks of his fellow lunatics, misfits and rejects in his old age at the end of *Amadeus*. The teenagers of the 1960s who reject and are rejected by an older generation in *Taking Off*, are no more lost or confused than their middle-American parents. It's circumstance that makes people what they are, not moral absolutes or fixed notions of right and wrong, good and bad. 'Milos Forman works with the ordinary, everyday reality of things,' says Jack Nicholson, morally ambiguous star of *One Flew Over the Cuckoo's Nest*.

It's as true of the glossy big budget productions of post-1968 as of the gentle, ironic humour of the comedies made in Czechoslovakia before Prague's New Wave cinema was rudely cut off by Russian tanks.

1968 found Forman in France, where *The Firemen's Ball* was representing Czechoslovakia. Despite its success with audiences who recognised themselves and their situation and welcomed the comic relief, trouble with a government that saw only an anti-government indictment of corruption and incompetence at

JUDITH VIDAL-HALL

Amadeus in Prague, 1984: genius, buffoon and outsider

the highest level ruled out return. A timely invitation to Hollywood snatched him from the path of the advancing tanks; back home, *The Firemen's Ball* was privately dubbed 'The last laugh in the face of the Russians.'

He was a reluctant exile: 'I was never a dissident, only a bit subversive. You do what you want or have to and other people stick on the labels.' And in odd counterpoint to the friend who stayed on, Jiří Menzel, adds, 'In any case I never thought it would be so long. Just a couple of films to prove I could make it out there. Who would have thought 22 years....' For the whole of which all his films, along with most of the irreverent New Wave, were banned, including *Amadeus*, the first and only film made in Prague since he left. 'They didn't want us, but we made them a financial offer — lots of hard currency — they couldn't refuse. Even so they treated us as though we didn't exist. The media were forbidden to mention us, the film wasn't shown until 1990. But everyone saw us filming in the streets; everybody was talking about it. That's the absurdity of censorship: people know what they are told they do not know.'

But Prague, after all, is the city of Kafka as well as Mozart. And as Forman himself says, Communism didn't invent the genre. Given his personal insights, had he never thought of filming Kafka? 'Frequently. It's not easy, but I think about it often.'

And might he return, permanently, to Prague? No. The decision was made a long time ago, in 1975 when he took US citizenship. While he talks with fond memories of old classmates like Vaclav Havel, or brilliant teachers like Milan Kundera, nostalgia is not enough. 'It's paralysing thinking all the time one day I'll go back. You don't do anything else.'

From nightmare to dream: Hollywood, America. What were the obvious differences? Weren't the constraints of the studio system and the tyranny of the market effectively more subtle variants on the old censorship? Not a bit of it. While working in Hollywood is not without its perils, its heady anxieties are a million miles from the old certainties of Communism.

'In Eastern Europe it was like being kept in a zoo: you were in a cage but there was a roof over your head and someone fed you every day. In the USA, it's the jungle: you're free to go where you like, but everyone's out there trying to kill you. In Communist countries there's a recipe, a formula for everything. There are no signs hung out in Hollywood. You make what people want to see and what market forces determine they want.' And while the much-maligned market has its own laws, they're a good deal easier to negotiate than political ideologies. Financing what the money men consider 'uncommercial' can be a problem, not a prohibition. Nor is it something that's suddenly loomed into the forefront as one might think from the griping in Europe and other parts of the world. 'Even back in 1975, a film like *One Flew Over the Cuckoo's Nest,* not on the face of it a commercial winner — an asylum for the mentally ill and misfits turned over by a guy who is supposedly criminally insane — eventually found a backer. It was made on a budget that looks derisory today, US$1.4 million because everyone involved did it for peanuts. Even so it came out at US$4 million. Then of course, it took off and everyone was happy.' Marketing, he says with the confidence of a 10-percenter, is for the mediocre; the 10 per cent that matter will make it anyway. 'There's not one, monolithic "Hollywood",' he reflects, 'more like one behind every door; find the right door.'

MILOS FORMAN

He blows away French fears that US cinema with its saturation marketing and global reach will wipe out the European industry, with the thought that competition not quotas — just another form of censorship — might provoke some quality films with specific national character and appeal rather than straining to join the Americans in the game they play best.

But doesn't he fear his America is under attack from the radical, new right? Government-hating militias, religious fundamentalists, disenchanted blacks, angry white males and extremists of all kinds? 'For years I've had huge faith in America. It's a self-correcting system: the pendulum swings way over to one side, and then rights itself. Look at McCarthy. It seemed as though it was the end of Hollywood. But no. I still have faith that the pendulum will right itself. America is condemned to freedom. The USA has more races, religions, languages than Yugoslavia. Why isn't there a permanent civil war? Freedom is the opposite of human stupidity. The day America forgets that it's in trouble.'

Forman has shown a prescient sense of timing with many of his films. *One Flew Over the Cuckoo's Nest* for instance. As well as picking up on the subversive, and at the time revolutionary, theories of R D Laing and others who reversed conventional thinking on sanity and society, it was a poignant commentary on the abuse of psychiatry in the Communist world where psychiatric hospitals became prisons for the mentally dissident.

But no: *People versus Larry Flint* is not a response to the growth of the radical right in the USA. The script was in the offing 'long before Gingrich and Dole got going on the big speeches'. But the tale of the sleazy purveyor of porn, outside the pale of 'decent' society winning a victory for the benefit of all Americans, could touch a chord. It's due to open around the time of the presidential elections; the stakes are higher than they've been for a long time.

Like many who were victims of film as propaganda and who as film-makers found themselves expected to produce the film with the right message rather than a personal meaning, Forman debunks 'the power of the movie', benign or otherwise. 'For a couple of hours I can be very powerful. Then audiences go out, life takes over. Film can have an effect, but something in life could achieve exactly the same effect. We most of us live vicariously. It's pure entertainment. There are only two things in life: living it and talking about it. All the rest is survival. People go to the movies to escape, to be entertained. The majority go to a movie to stave off boredom; there's only about 10 per cent who go for any real reason like seeing the work of a particular director or because they want to know what this film says.'

He talked about the flood of anti-heroes on the US screen, the Stallones, Schwarzeneggers, Willises, and found the cosy reassurance of *Forrest Gump* an interesting phenomenon. 'It's sentimental, well made and a healthy reaction: here's the common man and he's a hero. Americans are afraid; they don't know how to protect themselves from what they see around them and mirrored on the screen. Life and art become blurred. Look what the networks did with O J Simpson. The perfect drama: did he, didn't he; will they, won't they find him guilty. The lawyers are the heroes of the courtroom drama. The only solution people see is yet more guns: one in your pocket, one in mine. And calls to get tough on law and order.'

Aided and abetted by the image-makers of fact and fiction, society moves steadily to the right. And Hollywood is not much interested in eternal truths, only the eternal dream, all the better for being American. 'Telling the truth without being boring is difficult and people don't want to hear it anyway; lies are easier, more intriguing.' The secret of success for this film-maker lies in 'finding a truth that everyone knows and telling it in a way they haven't heard before'.

It's a line that holds for *People versus Larry Flint*. Every schoolchild knows by heart the rights and liberties promised under the Constitution; Americans everywhere still sing the praises of 'the land of the free'. It is under threat from politicians who offer to trade 'a little liberty for a little security' to a population frightened into forgetting what's at stake. And from extremists of all shades who, in the interests of one propaganda silence others, often, though not always, with the best intentions.

Maybe it needs an outsider who has lived most of his life without them and come to care for them so passionately to retell the USA what it knows so well: there is no liberty without free expression. Not by putting high sounding phrases into the mouth of an ancient constitutional grandee or right-on liberal campaigner, but through the modern history of *Hustler*. ❏

Interview by Sally Sampson and Judith Vidal-Hall

HAILE GERIMA

Images of Africa

'Censorship, for me, is political, economic and cultural. Most African film-makers feel that they were born at the wrong time and in the wrong place; and that's a terrible feeling for anyone who wants to express himself. It's OK if you are a dancer or writer, but with film, you need finance. Africa controls neither the capital nor the technology'

I don't have the material power to create a budget, but at least I can negotiate from my position within the Afro-American community in the USA. It is a sad thing to be born in a Third World country with so much to say and so few resources.

Few countries in Africa have a national policy on cinema: the more cinema is repressed, the better for those in power. As they say in South America, motion pictures are like a 'new hydrogen bomb': drop American movies by satellite on to a village, and that village will explode, culturally speaking. The cultural domination from outside is so strong that there is no chance of manufacturing local images.

In the francophone parts of Africa, film-makers follow a European notion of what African cinema is like; that is a kind of censorship. Instead of making a personal film about my grandmother, I'd ask myself, 'What do the French like? Something exotic!' There should be a national film policy to help African film-makers build up an archive of national memory.

Film-makers are trying to make their own personal films on video in Ghana; they will use any instrument to ingrain their humanity. This is happening in Mozambique and Ethiopia; it can be very powerful, especially if film-makers begin to realise their capacity to affect society, even if some of these videos are an imitation of *Dallas*, with some witchcraft thrown in for good measure.

In America, slavery is a very sensitive topic. The moment I wanted to make *Sankofa* (1993) my credentials in the USA vanished, because I was venturing into forbidden territory. The resource centres were closed to me: I couldn't get funding. Censorship became a reality; the funding agencies for cultural development shut their doors. They'd talk about timing: 'This year's budget is nearly spent. You're too late — or too early.' Nobody comes out with it straight and says that the subject matter is wrong. The press is much the same; they wouldn't touch *Sankofa* at Berlin, though it was in competition with big budget movies. They censor you by making you non-existent. We went to Montreal and Toronto: they skipped us, didn't even talk to us. They thought we were finished.

The film opened in Washington DC in a second-run theatre. None of the big distributors would touch it (one of them said it was 'too black'!) so we invited 20 activists from the community to see it. They opened a theatre, and the rest is history. The film was a smash hit with black people all over the country. In New York we were at the Cineplex, and got our money back. Now we're preparing a major launch on video, by mail order: we're demonstrating the marketability of the movie. Over 50,000 people in each city have signed to buy it.

Many African-Americans and Chicanos can't make the movies they want to make, because they don't live up to the expectations of white producers. That's why you see so

NATIONAL FILM THEATRE

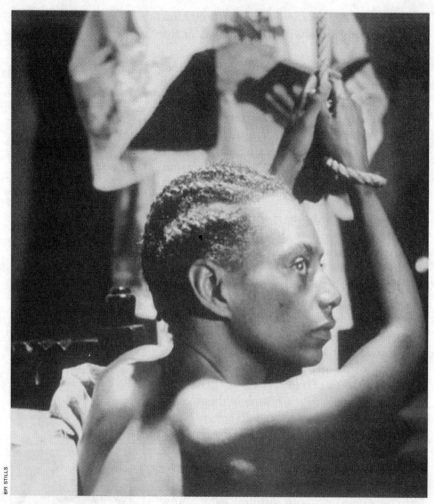

Sankofa, *1993: 'venturing into forbidden territory'*

BFI STILLS

many black independent film-makers playing in with Hollywood and making bizarre 'shoot 'em up and kill' movies. Black people respect Spike Lee, especially for his shrewd ability to function in that mega world; he brings many black talents into his productions. Our people see Spike walking the commercial tightrope to make something serious, and more dignified. He's at a critical stage now, and we are waiting to see what happens next.

Churches and schools came in busloads to see *Sankofa*; they are culturally hungry for a different kind of movie. Most black movies make black people look very bizarre, hopelessly bizarre; this is unacceptable. Commercial film-makers sometimes leave the community unfulfilled and demoralised, asking itself: 'Is this all that blacks are capable of?' Church people complain that the romanticism and glamour associated with violence in mainstream black films trickle back into the community. While Hollywood continues to select and produce films that reflect its own view of what the black community is, this contradiction will continue.

Sankofa may well be a milestone linking African cinema to African-American cinema. It is the first time two African countries, Ghana and Burkina Faso, have collaborated on a film about slavery. But to talk of African cinema is sometimes very hard: even Ousmane Sembene, the father of African social cinema, has to wait 10 to 15 years between films, and I know 20 film-makers in Ethiopia who have not made a film in five years. They think the world is against them, but they still want to effect change.

South Africa is crucial to the rest of Africa: it has the technology and the infrastructure. But this could be a two-edged sword: it will be a platform for the USA and the rest of the West. If it merely exploits this by pumping Hollywood movies and videotapes in a very sophisticated way all the way up from the Cape to North Africa, that could be frightening. But if South Africans develop their own cinema and create an easy working platform for film-makers all over Africa, in countries where there are no laboratories, this will be to the advantage of all of us. South Africa is a crossroads. ❏

Interviewed by Sally Sampson

ADEWALE MAJA-PEARCE

Made in Nigeria

At first sight, the Nigerian film industry appears relatively under-developed, especially when compared with its French-speaking neighbours, where subsidies from the French Ministry of Co-operation over the last 30 years have effectively generated an industry that couldn't survive on its own. In Nigeria, where there are no subsidies whatsoever; and where, furthermore, successive governments have actively shown themselves hostile to any manifestations of culture, there is nevertheless a thriving industry in indigenous-language films. Two of the three big language groups, Igbo and Yoruba, each of which has a minimum of 20 million speakers, are particularly well served.

The majority of these films are shot on video, which is about 30 per cent cheaper than celluloid; many are subtitled in English in order to broaden their appeal. The more successful films can sell upwards of 50,000 copies, although the country's poor infrastructure means that potential total sales are a long way from being realised. Other problems faced by the film companies include large-scale piracy in a country where police corruption makes a nonsense of the existing copyright laws; lack of properly trained technical staff; and the unhelpful attitude of an official bureaucracy incapable of taking decisions without reference to the top. As one film-maker pointed out, it can take up to three months to get permission to use a police station, which is why 'we are forced to confine ourselves to stories that touch the heart.' But even then there can be problems. Only recently, three actors were arrested in Lagos while shooting a film about armed robbers. The police, who didn't bother to listen to their explanation, claimed they mistook them for the real thing.

The majority of the indigenous-language films are straightforward narratives with an overt moral message. Among the current raves are *Thirst for Life* (Yoruba), the story of a wealthy businessman who decides that he deserves a younger and more beautiful wife in keeping with his new-found social status. Unfortunately, the new wife turns out to be a terror, and reduces him to a puppet in his own house. Another film, *Return to Paradise* (Igbo), is about a spoilt young woman who rebels against her wealthy parents, pays a heavy price for it, and meekly returns to the fold having learned the error of her ways. A third film, *Living Ghost* (Igbo), is about a man who enters into a pact with a ghost in return for wealth, only to discover that a condition of his success is that he marry a blind woman or forfeit his life. But perhaps the most popular film to date, *Living in Bondage* (Igbo), which was released in 1992, is the story of a young man who becomes dispirited because of his failure to make money. In desperation, he joins a secret cult, where he is told that he must sacrifice his wife. He achieves his aim but is driven mad by his conscience.

As the above examples demonstrate, the films themselves reflect rather than examine the prevailing mores of Nigerian society. A film like *Living Ghost*, for instance, assumes as a matter of course that physically disabled people are unworthy recipients of disinterested love, especially by young men on the make. Similarly, *Return to Paradise*, which merely guarantees the authoritarian, patriarchal nature of a society where young women, however well-educated, are punished for challenging their elders and betters, fails to make the connection between rigid social convention and the on-going political dispensation in which tyranny has been permitted to prevail — by decree. Authority, in other words, is its own justification, is not to be challenged and the attempt to do so can only end in disaster.

The film-makers might object that they are merely providing entertainment, which is true enough as far as it goes, the problem being that such a view is rendered impossible in a society where all forms of cultural expression are a matter of politics, as the authorities themselves have demonstrated time and again. A case in point is Eddie Ugbomah's *The Great Attempt*, which was released in the mid-1980s. On the surface at least, a film which concerned itself with the machinations of a foreign power, in this case the USA, attempting to undermine the Nigerian economy for its own selfish ends, might be taken as an expression of patriotism on the part of the artist. However, as Ugbomah recounts: '[The National Censors Board] had to bring in the Central Bank for any word said about the Central Bank; [they brought in] the State Security Service (SSS) who insisted that I must cut this or that... No, they said, why should I show five SSS people of whom one is corrupt? Nobody is corrupt in the SSS. Why should I show the police drinking beer? No policeman drinks beer... Now they're telling me to bring the film back because they've called somebody from external affairs to determine whether the film might annoy the US. But the US can show Tarzan beating...black people...'

The idea that the government and people of the USA might be remotely concerned with the simplistic (not to say tendentious) politics of a film they will almost certainly never see is interesting only for what it conveys about the pitiful spiritual condition of those who are entrusted to make judgements concerning what is and isn't suitable fare for the viewing public. But Eddie Ugbomah is one of the few overtly political film-makers in the country willing to test the boundaries of the politically acceptable. The majority of Nigerian film-makers appear only too willing to do 'most of the censorship ourselves' in order to get their films passed with the minimum of fuss, which in turn raises the question of their moral authority to make films about businessmen who sell their souls for a mess of pottage.

In any case, Nigerian society provides more than enough evidence that crime does indeed pay; worse yet, it has consistently demonstrated that pretensions to probity are the surest route to penury — or worse. Another politically-conscious film-maker, writer and activist, Ken Saro-Wiwa, has been in detention on a dubious murder charge since May last year for attempting to expose the genocidal tendencies of the present military administration (see *Index*, 4&5/94, see also below, pp164). A recent British television documentary about the plight of Saro-Wiwa and the Ogoni people, whose basic human rights he is fighting for, will almost certainly never be shown on Nigerian television. We might even be tempted to ask why a foreign company should be doing our work for us, but such is the pitiful spiritual condition of Nigerian society and all those who are forced to function within it. ❏

SPIKE LEE

Clockers

Lee in Clockers, *New York, 1995*

UNIVERSAL STUDIOS

Clockers, Lee's latest movie, 'deals with the proliferation of violence and guns in our society, how movies, television, radio, music videos, gangsta rap, malt liquor ads — how this whole culture promotes carrying Uzis and nine millimeters.' For Lee, *Clockers* was an opportunity to capture the diversity of those who live within the confines of the [housing] projects. 'It would be a fallacy to say everyone in the projects is on dope or pregnant at 13. We wanted to show the humanity that these people have — and it's something that you might not necessarily see looking at the six o'clock news.'

MARJORIE HEINS

Gina Gershon and Elizabeth Berkley in Showgirls, *1995*

From X to N-17

Film ratings in the United States are controlled by the Motion Picture Association of America (MPAA), a private trade organisation representing the major film studios. The system operates through a separate industry organisation called the Classification and Rating Administration (CARA), but the MPAA's president selects the chair of the CARA ratings board and, with him, chooses the 'average American parents' who actually decide the ratings. The MPAA president also chairs the ratings appeals board. The actual process of classifying films with the G, PG, PG-13, R, and NC-17 ratings is not subject to public scrutiny.

Though marketed as 'consumer information', the rating system is in effect a form of censorship. To achieve the rating considered desirable by studios, film artists have routinely had to remove dialogue or even whole scenes from their work. US audiences rarely know what they're missing, except if they happen to catch the unexpurgated version of the movie playing in Europe or perhaps on a video-cassette.

To be sure, in the American economic system the studio that finances a movie controls its content. Film artists may be hard put to argue that they are being censored when their studio simply insists on certain changes, any more than a reporter can complain if her editor dislikes her story — or an author, if her publisher refuses to print her book without substantial editing.

But the line between editorial control and censorship begins to blur when it's not an individual production company but a powerful industry-wide consortium that makes the rules. It is the monopolistic nature of the MPAA system, the hold that the industry maintains over the economic means to market a film in the United States, that renders the ratings a form of censorship rather than simply an exercise in editorial judgement. Many theatres in the US refuse to show an NC-17 film, and many newspapers and radio and television stations will not carry advertising for one. Blockbuster Video, Kmart and Walmart, which account for more than half of the video sales in the US, will not handle NC-17 titles.

Government agencies, particularly school boards and libraries, are increasingly relying upon the industry ratings to set official policy for access by minors to films and videos. Yet the ratings have no legal status, are arrived at in relative secret, and are not subject to review by any court. To incorporate these amorphous and subjective judgements into law is at odds with US constitutional principles of both artistic freedom and due process.

The internal workings of the rating system came to light during a lawsuit filed in 1990 by Miramax Films and the popular Spanish director Pedro Almodóvar. They challenged the X rating that CARA had given to Almodóvar's *Tie Me Up, Tie Me Down*, an arguably misogynistic comedy about a kidnap victim who falls in love with her attacker.

Technically, the MPAA and CARA won the Miramax case. But in the course of his decision, New York State Judge Charles Ramos expressed considerable disgust at the hypocrisy and arbitrariness of the ratings, saying that he wouldn't 'dignify the present system by rendering an opinion on so frivolous a standard as the wishes of the AAP' (that is, the 'average American parent,' the MPAA board's professed guideline). Judge Ramos described the rating system as 'an effective form of censorship'.

The record reveals that films are produced and *negotiated* to fit the ratings. After an initial X rating of a film whole scenes or parts thereof are cut in order to fit within the R category. Contrary to our jurisprudence, which protects all forms of expression, the rating system censors serious films by the force of economic pressure.

Not long after the Miramax case, the MPAA changed the name for its X rating to the less loaded NC-17. But the new label did not — until very recently — save films with the pejorative rating from likely economic doom.

Even a superstar like Madonna was hard put to fight the ratings. In late 1992 her steamy film, *Body of Evidence*, was cut to avoid the dreaded NC-17. Because *Body of Evidence* was intended for mass marketing, not an art film crowd, the producer considered it 'crucial that it be acceptable to exhibitors throughout the country'. Likewise, French director Louis Malle, after initially refusing to make changes when his film, *Damage*, drew an NC-17 in late 1992, ultimately was forced to capitulate to cuts. Malle reacted with astonishment:

'It's unbelievable! Why does this country have such a strange taboo about nudity? They don't care about ice-picks slashed into the chests of lovers like *Basic Instinct*. ...I find it sometimes weird here.'

But the willingness of directors like Malle and companies like Miramax to buck the system offered some hope of loosening the rating system's grip. In September 1995, the NC-17-rated *Showgirls* broke the system's economic stranglehold by receiving major bookings nationwide in commercial movie houses, and reaping hefty profits in its first week. If theatres remain willing to show unrated or NC-17-rated films, the censorship power of the rating system will undoubtedly diminish.

Such a development would hardly leave the public bereft of information about the content of movies. The MPAA's letter ratings offer precious little such information to begin with. Reviews, coming attractions, promotions, ads, and guides circulated by religious and other groups are all more useful sources. Yet, even if the rating system loses its power to force film-makers to censor their work in deference to the MPAA's 'average American parent', it is likely that some ingenious new system will rise in its place, given the apparently eternal human urge to censor. ❏

BERTRAND TAVERNIER

ARTIFICIAL EYE

The case for quotas

Why do you say that American market forces act as a kind of censorship of foreign films in the United States?

The total of the entire world cinema shown in the United States — German, Japanese, Spanish, British, Russian — is less than two per cent. In France, even with the quota imposed by the government, the total of films from other countries is 50 per cent. And they accuse us of protectionism! Americans don't buy foreign books. They don't listen to foreign songs. As Wim Wenders says, among all civilised countries, the US is the one where the lowest percentage of people own a passport. Ignorance is the worst protectionism in the world.

Would your objections be answered if the US market were more open to films from other countries; if there was a quota there as well?

But that's impossible! How could you do that? Maybe if some cable TV companies took more foreign material... Ted Turner has talked about buying cable channels in Europe. What if he bought a percentage of European films to show on his American cable channels? If he can do something like his TNT Classics channel, which shows old Hollywood films, why shouldn't his channel in Europe include 30 per cent or 40 per cent of European films? That should be normal. We give him something — a market for his product. Against that, we should get something. It should be the duty of the European Parliament and the European Commission in Brussels to fix that. And from that, we could dream — and Turner has implied this — that he would be ready to finance and co-finance a series of films. We have to be suspicious — there's always the risk they would be pseudo-European films. But such an arrangement seems perfectly natural.

Why is the US market so hostile to foreign films? Is it an official policy?

There had never been an *official* law barring non-US films. Jack Valenti [outgoing head of the Motion Picture Association of America, and for some years the White House's voice on American film] always said, 'Look, we don't have any law against non-American films.' This was said a lot by the Americans [during the GATT negotiations] at Brussels. But if you study the history of the cinema, you will discover there is such a law, though unwritten. It goes back to the turn of the century, when the cameramen of the Lumière brothers who tried to demonstrate their equipment were physically thrown out of the USA by the representatives of Thomas Edison. Actually thrown into boats and forced to leave.

Mr Valenti has said many times that the American audience doesn't want to see subtitled films and it doesn't want to see dubbed films either. With an attitude like that, you don't need any official protectionism!

What do you think would happen if French cinema suddenly began to enjoy a vogue in the USA? Do you feel that the US government would impose a quota?

We told the Americans: 'You say you oppose quotas, but you imposed them on Japanese cars. And now you are talking of doing the same against imported pasta.' And to this, they respond: 'Well, nobody's perfect.' But we're not even dreaming of being so successful! What we would like is that the percentage of non-American cinema shown in the USA would represent, say, three per cent instead of two per cent. That's our dream. When we met the people of the major companies and we said, 'Look, how can you accuse France of protectionism when foreign films don't even represent two per cent of your market?', we saw surprise in their eyes. You could see them thinking, 'two per cent — as much as that? How can we arrange things so that they have only one-and-a-half per cent?'

What do you feel about the attitude of the US press to foreign films? Because presumably, if a film is well reviewed, it will win an audience, no matter what the government says.

I feel there's a protectionist trend in the American press too. There's less and less space being given to foreign films in many magazines and newspapers. David Thomson, one of the best American critics, can admit that he's never seen a film by [Japanese 1930s director] Mikio Naruse. Leonard Maltin's latest encyclopaedia includes Winona Ryder but has no mention of Julien Duvivier.

Some critics who knew about European cinema have retired. Others have moved to papers that don't give so much space to cinema. Kevin Thomas, on the *Los Angeles Times*, a specialist in foreign films, is now the paper's fourth or fifth film critic. There was a time when one of my films had a whole page in *Newsweek*. Jacques Rivette, Bertrand Blier and many others were the same. But these days, *Time* and *Newsweek* devote a lot of space to new US films just to say they're junk!

One of the most common charges against the campaign being waged for protection of the French cinema is chauvinism. Half all foreign films shown in America are French; aren't you just looking out for yourselves?

What we want is the possibility of survival. We don't want to prevent other people from making films. We want to keep our system, which helps a certain kind of film — and not only French films. We make a lot of co-productions. Angelopoulos, Kustarica, Jane Campion, Kieślowski, Mikhalkov, the new Mike Leigh, to name only a few. Fellini's last films were all co-produced by France. If we had not been there, there would not have been any Fellini films. It's not just protecting French cinema. It's protecting one kind of cinema, the cinema of Fellini, of Kieślowski, of Kuleshov, of Rivette, of Godard, against, let's say, Schwarzenegger, Bruce Willis, against *Die Hard* and *Indiana Jones*. It's to have other alternatives.

US films still dominate the French domestic market. How can you justify maintaining a cinema that people don't want to see?

We are living in hard times. There is such an atmosphere of crisis that people don't want to see films based on doubt — most European films. If I wanted to be simplistic, I'd say that European cinema is based on doubt and questions, and the American cinema is based on affirmation. And in a period of crisis, people want to see more affirmative films. People in the suburbs would rather see *Die Hard 51* than the new Mike Leigh film. Of course, if things were better, maybe Mike Leigh would be making more optimistic films. Or maybe not making films at all.

It's not only films either. Books, newspapers and magazines are all suffering; never isolate the cinema from other media — it's only one parcel of a culture. The French cinema is surviving much better than French newspapers. I'm always quoting the fact that there was a page in a French daily with the headline 'The New French Cinema Disaster'. Well, two weeks later, that daily ceased to exist. But we're still here. If we want to have hope, we can remember that for the first screening of the Lumière brothers in 1895, there were only 23 people. So the French cinema was already in crisis, even then.

In the USA the major studios argue that, in such hard times, they would be failing their shareholders if they didn't maximise profits by taking control of film studios and theatre chains in other countries.

Maybe that was true once, but the attitudes of the American majors are changing. They see now that there are ways to make a profit and allow other national cinemas to survive. One example we gave when we had lunch with the people of the MPAA: when there was an Italian cinema and it had 50 per cent or 55 per cent of the Italian market, the American major companies were making more money [through distribution of their films, and with co-productions] than now, when they own 70 per cent or 80 per cent of the market. They are discovering that they must encourage national cinema, because it brings them more money.

This isn't new. Paramount did some films in France with Claude Sautet. Most of Truffaut's films were produced by Warner or United Artists. My own *Que la Fête Commence* (Let Joy Reign Supreme) was backed by Hollywood. If the majors were helping three or four national films every year, it would give a new energy, and it would be beneficial both to them and to world cinema. And to fight for the films of the past on cable and the films of the present in the cinema is the same fight. It has one goal: to increase the curiosity of the viewer, to increase his desire to see films, to increase his knowledge and his appetite.

Your latest film, L'Appât *(The Bait), has stirred up some controversy. You based it on a true story of three Parisian teenagers who committed murder in the hope of going to the USA and opening a clothing store. It's been widely seen as your attack on US values.*

No, it's an attack against a certain kind of image — which can be an American image or a French image — and not on the American cinema. The films seen by the people of *L'Appât*, which are mostly TV films, represent only one side of the American cinema. It's more an attack on the American Dream, and people here in France who are victims of the American Dream. They have no link with the society and the country in which they live, and they believe in the image of success delivered by US films. But it's very clear in the film that they have absolutely no knowledge of the USA. It's the story of three people who want to be very successful in the USA, but who don't speak English. It's as if these people have no antibodies, if you like, to protect them from the effect of these films. These antibodies could be political, social or religious involvement, moral values, trade unionism, knowing the society; knowledge, curiosity — anything like that. They don't have that. So it's like a virus against which they have no antibodies. ❑

Interview by John Baxter

GEOFFREY WOOD

A censor's tale

By the time I left the British Board of Film Classification in 1994, life there had assumed a strange double quality: justifying film censorship to those outside, struggling for basic freedoms inside. While there is a place for film and video censorship, the BBFC is at a point where fundamental reforms must be made if it is any longer to be trusted. Far from being rendered redundant in the face of the information super-highway, informed public discussion about the politics of visual images in our culture is even more vital.

The word 'censorship' is used too casually as a synonym for political repression. There are important distinctions between cutting a rape or torture scene from a pornographic film, and the imprisonment of an artist or journalist for his or her work. Film censorship is only one of a number of interventions made in the course of the product's progress from studio to screen and many screenwriters and directors have ruefully described how corporate decisions have changed their work or their intentions. By the time a film arrives at the BBFC there will already have been production and distribution decisions: I have viewed a film or video at the BBFC that has been drastically cut by the British distributor; and there have even been cases where a video has been so hacked about that we have suggested reinstating footage in the interests of artistic viability. The effect of using preview audiences often alters a film considerably; and, of course, more draconian cuts are made for television viewing than any made by the BBFC. If the concern is for integrity of product, there are other villains than censorship. What *is* different about film censorship is that it acts as a moral regulator on behalf of the state in otherwise unregulated markets.

A major argument often made by those who attack the idea of film censorship, is that it is best left to the law to decide questions of obscenity. But the law can only be retrospective, shutting the stable door after the horse has gone since videos can easily be sold and copied before a prosecution. Further, the law on obscenity refers to 'the tendency to deprave and corrupt', something that might better apply to the frequency of certain images or scenarios than to a single work; the rape-turning-to-consent scenario in 1970s pornography is an example. This more subtle distinction is difficult for the law to police. In addition, the fear and expense of litigation might have an adverse effect on more venturesome projects with lawyers advising caution. The BBFC provides a comparatively cheap testing of the waters and an umbrella against litigious storms. And finally, unlike the practice at the BBFC under its present director, James Ferman, aesthetic and ethical discrimination and appreciation of film styles and genres seem to be low priorities in the few cases that have come to court for obscenity.

The most obvious cases for censorship, apart from child pornography and racism, are scenes of sexual violence offered solely for titillation. One worry about corruption is that such images may become banal rather than shocking. Desensitisation is a particularly pertinent problem for the film censor: for the most part, the material is fairly innocuous, and one of the first requirements for the job is the ability to put up with a vast amount of stereotyped and vacuous material. But one can also become inured to blood in horror videos and see sex, as depicted on the screen, as one of the most banal of activities. I don't know if this causes psychic damage, but one guard against it is professional rigour, another should be that the job be part-time and examiners drawn from a wide range of occupations, with a wide experience of life and work outside censorship. My colleagues included teachers, psychotherapists, magistrates, a film producer and a choreographer as well as several writers. Most of us were parents. Having young children gave me food for thought on the difficulties of a mandatory rather than recommendatory system of age-categories. There is already an element of conservatism in the British system and though children need to be protected from horrific images, they are often more resilient than their parents like to think.

It is not entirely clear where the censor's responsibilities lie, especially after the Video Recordings Act 1984 and the clauses on video censorship in the 1994 Criminal Justice Act. The current director describes the Board's work as a 'service industry' for the film and video industries, reminding us that the BBFC was an independent body set up by the film industry in 1912 to protect it from the state and to protect individual companies from prosecution. But since 1984 the BBFC has a legal responsibility to the state in addition to certain undefined responsibilities to the public. Most decisions within the BBFC are based on a set of guidelines (unpublished), but procedures are skewed towards an authoritarian mode. Examples of its operation since 1993 include the holding up of films like *The Good Son* and *Natural Born Killers*, and videos such as *Reservoir Dogs*. The warning signs for examiners had come years earlier when *The Texas Chainsaw Massacre 2* was excised from Board debate. This was followed by a running battle on *The Exorcist* when it suddenly transpired that the distributor had asked a number of times over the years if a video version could be submitted and had repeatedly been told to wait. Examiners had not been told of this and subsequent viewing and discussions became a war of attrition fought through monthly board meetings. The vast majority of examiners were in favour of passing it on video, but there was no action.

Examiners had fought for many years for reform: democratic decision-making and the establishment of a constitution ensuring consistency and openness. A Review Committee finally established to question any disputed or difficult decisions and report before the full board — a check on both examiners and management — went largely ignored by management. When James Ferman was appointed chief censor in 1975, he brought new standards of viewing and reporting to the Board; but by the mid-1980s, it was stuck in an unfinished revolution. Backed by a newly appointed presidential troika, the directors word became law: Ferman could do what he liked. What he did at the end of 1993 was to sack his recalcitrant Board in toto.

By this time, examiners had become little more than lower level bureaucrats sifting material for reference to a higher, smaller cabal of decision-makers. By 1995, the censors' life had become even more restricted: less money and short-term contracts that were full-time, leaving little room for the breadth and variety of experience that characterised the Board a decade earlier.

It is the business of government not simply to produce guidelines for quangoes but charters laying down proper procedures, transparency and control in organisations such as the BBFC. It is the role of a wider public to push for such changes, still within the framework of a regulatory body, but one separate from government and bureaucracy. The Board needs to transform itself from Sun King to a more open and accountable body. ❑

JOHN SAYLES

How to stay independent

'If you're clear that the point is the work itself, not the economic gains or celebrity glory, you have the necessary focus to try at least to tell a movie story with an independence of spirit'

In the mainstream US film industry, anything produced and distributed by anyone other than the major studios (Fox, Warners, Universal, MGM-UA, Sony-Tristar, Disney, Columbia, Paramount) is considered independent. It may star Arnold Schwarzenegger and cost US$80 million, but by *Variety* standards, it is 'independent' of the studio machinery.

When we first started to make movies in the late 1970s, early 1980s, there was a move by organisations such as the Independent Feature Project to define independent films in terms of subject matter as well; to separate them in some way from porno, kung-fu, horror and other 'exploitation' films. In the last six or seven years, many of the most highly regarded movies at festivals and on the art circuit have been squarely within, or on the border of, these exploitation genres and have used actors familiar from mainstream studio films, so that definition has faded. Faced with a class of films that can include *The Brothers McMullen, A Room with a View, Beneath the Valley of the Ultravixens* and *I Dismember Mama*, I prefer to consider the spirit in which the film was made rather than the financial mechanisms through which it was produced and distributed.

Marketing plays a huge part in the film industry, as in other US mass-market businesses. Major studios regularly run market-testing screenings of their films, not only to study how to sell them, but how to tell the story — cuts are made, endings changed or reshot, depending on the responses of the test audiences. Even without test marketing, a great deal of thought goes into how to please a certain demographic of the audience — what to cast, what is too controversial, what is sexy enough to get men and boys interested but mainstream enough to obtain an R or PG rather than an NC-17 rating. Some very good movies are made by this process, and some of them are commercially successful. But the driving force is to sell a product, not to tell a story. Many good movies are ruined or irreparably watered down for purely commercial reasons — guesses by the people with the final say as to what will sell.

The other method of making a movie is to have a story in mind and then do everything in your power to get it made without compromising its quality. It doesn't matter what genre it's in, whether the financing of the production is from a studio or not, the driving force is to tell that story as well as is possible. Every decision — casting, location, music, editing — is based on maximising the potential of the story to do its work — entertain, instruct, terrify, whatever — with the implicit belief that if you make a good movie somebody will pay to see it. A guy who owns a chain of parking garages who sinks US$200,000 into a low-budget mood piece, can be just as meddling and box-office obsessed as a room full of studio executives — and usually with less talent and experience.

A great number of movies lie between these two extremes — producers, writers, directors who have a story they believe in and are willing to do battle for, but no way of financing it without giving up a certain amount of control. The compromises they make range from the merely cosmetic to situations where 'we had to destroy the village in order to save it.' People start out in Hollywood making compromises in search of the huge financial hit that will buy them the power to call the shots creatively the next time out. A few achieve this, a few become 'the object of their former contempt', and most struggle along like most people do in life, making the best of a tough situation, choosing when to take a stand and when to retreat.

So, how to stay independent? We've made 10 movies now, and the compromises I've had to make on them have all been economic rather than aesthetic. I have a source of income separate from directing movies — I am a screenwriter for hire, helping other people tell *their* story and getting very well paid for it. I've been a major investor in about half our movies, sometimes the sole one, and generally don't pay myself as director and editor, only Writers Guild scale for the screenplay. I don't have kids, don't have an exorbitantly lavish lifestyle to maintain, so I've been able (and willing) to put all my earnings on the line for a project. Sometimes I've gotten it back, sometimes not. I don't live in the film community in Hollywood or New York where the value system is unavoidably tied up with the weekend box-office grosses and the Monday television ratings. We've gotten better and better at putting out 'a polished product' on a relatively low budget. Because we've retained control over our movies we can often attract actors to work for less than their usual rates — the attraction being that they deal with me personally, not with a committee of executives or a marketing focus group. We are willing to walk away from the wrong money. If it is clear that a financier expects more control, more 'input', than you are willing to give up, you start from scratch and look for money elsewhere. When we do strike a deal, creative control issues are explicitly covered in the contract. We have had rocky marriages with investors but have never lost control of the story-telling. We try to be responsible with the budget and with the expectations of our investors. Like leaving a campsite in order for the next traveller, we hope our financiers know exactly what they're gambling on and don't feel cheated if the movie isn't a hit. We have resigned ourselves not to expect immediate gratification. *Matewan* took eight years to get off the ground; *Eight Men Out* took 11. None of our movies were made in the order in which I wrote them. This is often discouraging and depressing, but the upside is that you really have to want to make the movie. Not to 'be a director', which is something different, but to make that particular story in a situation where it can come out the way you want it. So when somebody dangles the financing in front of you if you'll use a certain actor who is wrong for the lead, you don't think twice before thanking them and saying no.

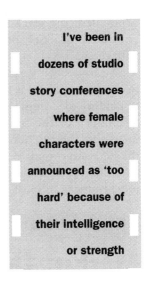

I've been in dozens of studio story conferences where female characters were announced as 'too hard' because of their intelligence or strength

We have never had a huge box-office hit that guaranteed us financing for our next feature. All our movies have gotten theatrical distribution, sometimes efficient, sometimes half-hearted. More than half the people who see our movies see them on video, and there are entire states where we don't show in a single theatre. We don't make movies for 'a handful of our friends', because we don't have a million friends, but we very clearly don't aim at the widest demographic group of movie-goers.

Economic censorship is much stronger in the US than the statutory laws. Studios limit the sexual content of their films because many big city newspapers and TV stations won't run ads for NC-17 films and they don't think they'll make as big a profit without that mass-market advertising. A self-censorship based on economics sets in. I've been in dozens of studio story conferences where female characters were announced as 'too hard' because of their intelligence or strength. When confronted, the story editors never claimed to have a personal problem with these qualities, only that 'the general audience' was uncomfortable with them.

We have been very lucky. Movies are expensive to make, complicated to distribute. There is no way to make movies that are seen in more than a handful of commercial theatres and be totally independent of the machinery of the mainstream movie industry. But you don't have to internalise their values. If you're clear that the point is the work itself, not the economic gains or celebrity glory that might procede from it, you have the focus necessary to at least try to tell a movie story with an independence of spirit. ❏

KEN LOACH
Market takes all

The most serious form of censorship is indirect, via the market, where selection is made purely on commercial criteria. This automatically excludes those films which attempt to raise controversial topics or discuss serious issues. It is equally exclusive of relationships — between a director and financier say — that are not seen as commercial or potentially profitable.

Ireland is an important case in point. In itself, Ireland has all the ingredients film-makers look for: conflict, drama, tragedy, comedy. But the films that could explore all this have not been made because Ireland

ARTIFICIAL EYE

Land and Freedom, 1995: faced no problems with the censors

is thought to be 'uncommercial'; it turns people off — or so they say.

Let me cite just one example of an important subject judged to be off limits by the commercial world. Our film *Hidden Agenda* is about the British presence in Ireland and the corrupting effects of this on the British as well as on the Irish. Yet, before it had even been shown in Britain, it was pilloried in the right-wing press. There was a story in the *Daily Mail*, for instance, in which a Tory MP was quoted as saying it was an 'IRA film' with absolutely no substantiating evidence. Anything on Ireland seen as critical of government at the time was accused of being 'pro-IRA'. As a result, cinemas in the UK chose not to screen it. It came out about the time of the Gulf War and one cinema owner said she 'preferred not to show anything critical of British troops.'

When *Hidden Agenda* was submitted to the Cannes film festival in 1990, a group of right-wing journalists went to Cannes and asked for it to be withdrawn. While the director of the festival refused categorically to withdraw the film, the message that got back to Britain was that 'this is not the sort of film that should be representing our country abroad.'

Everything that could go wrong went wrong with *Hidden Agenda* — and at the same time. Our latest film, *Land and Freedom*, jointly financed by British Screen, Spain and Germany had no problems with censorship in Spain or anywhere else.

Cinema is part of the fabric of the world we live in; it contributes to our perceptions of that world and is part of a cultural ambience. If cinema really could influence people directly, it would be a distinctly malign force. What we'd be most likely to see would be Americans with guns solving problems by force.

Film can lodge a few thoughts, ideas in people's minds, that's all. Broadcasting has much more influence.

ARTHUR C CLARKE

Stanley Kubrick's 2001: A Space Odyssey, *1968: no hiding space*

Beyond 2001

It has always seemed to me that the limits of censorship are defined by two famous quotations: Voltaire's 'I disagree with everything you say — but will fight to the death for your right to say it' and Chief Justice Holmes's: 'Freedom of speech does not include the liberty to shout FIRE! in a crowded theatre.' In real life, one must attempt to steer a course between these two extremes. Thus I can tolerate astrologers purveying their (usually) harmless nonsense, but not anti-Semites and neo-Nazis hawking their poison. Even here, though, there is a fringe area: should Leni Riefenstahl's brilliant documentaries be banned because of their sponsor? And aren't there some rather embarrassing bits in *Birth of a Nation*?

As it happens, I have helped to destroy one form of censorship. Quoting from the speech I made at the UN on World Telecommunications Day, 17 May 1983, I pointed out that the development of communications satellites accessible by cheap and portable equipment would mean that 'news gatherers would no longer be at the mercy of censors or inefficient (sometimes non-existent) postal and telegraph services. It means the end of the closed societies and will lead ultimately — to repeat a phrase I heard Arnold Toynbee use 40 years ago — to the unification of the world.'

> What I am saying is that the debate about the free flow of information which has been going on for so many years will soon be settled — by engineers, not politicians. (Just as physicists, not generals, have now determined the nature of war.)
>
> Consider what this means. No government will be able to conceal, at least for very long, evidence of crimes or atrocities — even from its own people. The very existence of the myriads of new information channels, operating in real time and across all frontiers, will be a powerful influence for civilised behaviour. If you are arranging a massacre, it will be useless to shoot the cameraman who has so inconveniently appeared on the scene. His pictures will already be safe in the studio 5,000 kilometres away; and his final image may hang you.
>
> Many governments will not be at all happy about this, but in the long run everyone will benefit. Exposures of scandals or political abuses — especially by visiting TV teams who go home and make rude documentaries — can be painful but also very valuable. Many a ruler might still be in power today, or even alive, had he known what was really happening in his own country. A wise statesman once said, 'A free press can give you hell; but it can save your skin.' That is even more true of TV reporting — which, thanks to satellites, will soon be instantaneous and ubiquitous.

That was written more than 12 years ago: the satellite TV news gives hourly proof that this state of affairs has now arrived. Living as I do in Asia, I can also observe the impact of western movies and TV serials upon societies with totally different cultural backgrounds.

Sometimes it is hard not to sympathise with latter-day Canutes attempting to hold back the waves pouring down from the sky; what has been aptly called 'electronic imperialism' will sweep away much that is good, as well as much that is bad. Yet it will only accelerate changes that were in any case inevitable and, on the credit side, the new media will preserve for future generations the customs, performing arts and ceremonies of our time in a way that was never possible in any earlier age.

Recently I had the enjoyable task of using satellite links to address both Rupert Murdoch and Ted Turner (though not simultaneously!). I gave them this advice on the use and misuse of satellite TV. After quoting a British prime minister's famous accusation that the press enjoyed 'the privilege of the harlot — power without responsibility', I added:

Today, the TV screen is more powerful than newsprint, and whatever the bean-counters may say, responsibility should always be the bottom line.

Though I'm opposed in principle to any form of censorship, my stomach is often turned by the hideous violence shown on so many TV programmes. It's no excuse to say that Hollywood[*] is an even worse offender, and I know all the arguments about screen violence providing catharsis, and not role models. But you can't have it both ways: if the advertisers really believed that, they'd never buy any air time.

I don't believe that a civilisation can advance technologically without corresponding moral progress; if they get out of step, it will self-destruct, as ours is in danger of doing.

Which leads me to an awesome conclusion. We've had TV for 50 years. Therefore a volume of space containing several hundred suns has now been filled with news of our wars, atrocities and crimes — real ones and fictional ones, which an alien intelligence might have great difficulty in distinguishing.

I conclude from this that there's no, repeat no, superior civilisation in our immediate vicinity. For if there was — the cops would already be here, sirens screaming right across the radio spectrum.

To sum up: as this century draws to a close, it looks as if all the old arguments about censorship will be made obsolete by wide-band, person-to-person communications. When you can download anything and everything 'in the privacy of your own home', as certain notorious advertisements used to say, not even entire armies of Thought Police will be able to do anything about it.

The real challenge now facing us through the Internet and the World Wide Web is not quality but sheer quantity. How will we find anything

Director Kubrick and author Clarke on the set of 2001

— and not merely our favourite porn — in the overwhelming cyberbabble of billions of humans and trillions of computers, all chattering simultaneously?

I don't know the answer: and I have a horrible feeling that there may not be one. ❏

© Arthur C Clarke 1995

*And though Hollywood may be the worst offender, it is by no means the only one. I am reminded that *A Clockwork Orange* was made in England; the only time I ever saw it was when Stanley Kubrick arranged a screening for me at the studio. Although I understand that he has now withdrawn it from exhibition, later highly praised movies have been far more violent, with far less justification.

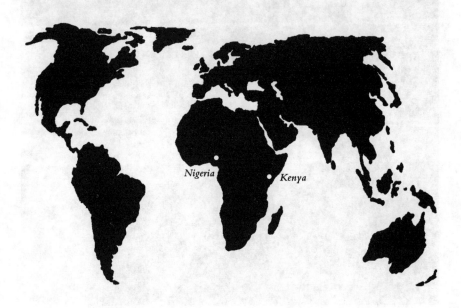

Nigeria   *Kenya*

Ordeal by innocence

By employing a clumsy bit of legal footwork, Kenya deftly avoided the embarrassment of having to put its leading dissident to death at the start of October. Koigi wa Wamwere and four other members of his National Democratic Human Rights Organisation (*Index* 2/1995, p17) have been on trial for the past 20 months, charged under the Hanging Act with armed robbery on a police station. At the very last minute, however, the judge started to play a different tune: the capital charge was inexplicably replaced by one of simple robbery. A guilty verdict passed, the sentence of four years in prison and six lashes of the cane was duly handed down.

Ken Saro-Wiwa is Nigeria's leading dissident and campaigner against the government's genocidal policy towards the Ogoni people. He, too, is on trial for his life, on a grotesquely fanciful charge of incitement to murder. A verdict is expected on 31 October, the day after *Index* goes to press. It's hard to foretell what verdict Nigeria's idiosyncratic justice system will come up with, but most observers believe Saro-Wiwa will be found guilty and sentenced to death, but that General Abacha, in a magnanimous show of clemency, will commute that to a custodial sentence. The fact that Abacha can expect a hard ride from his principal trading partners over his human rights record at November's Commonwealth heads of government meeting could prove a more powerful motive than any disinterested concern for Saro-Wiwa's well-being.

The following is an extract from a statement that Saro-Wiwa was prevented from reading out in court last month.

Adam Newey

'My lord, we all stand before history. I am a man of peace, of ideas. Appalled by the denigrating poverty of my people who live on a richly endowed land, distressed by their political marginalisation and economic strangulation, angered by the devastation of their land, anxious to preserve their right to life and to a decent living, and determined to usher to this country as a whole a fair and just democratic system, I have devoted all my intellectual and material resources — my very life — to a cause in which I have total belief and from which I cannot be blackmailed or intimidated. I have no doubt at all about the ultimate success of my cause, no matter the trials and tribulations which I and those who believe with me may encounter on our journey. Nor imprisonment nor death can stop our ultimate victory.

'I repeat that we all stand before history. I and my colleagues are not the only ones on trial. Shell is on trial here, and it is as well that it is represented by counsel said to be holding a watching brief. The company has, indeed, ducked this particular trial, but its day will surely come and the lessons learnt here may prove useful to it, for there is no doubt in my mind that the ecological war the company has waged in the delta will be called to question sooner than later and the crimes of that war be duly punished. The crime of the company's dirty wars against the Ogoni people will also be punished.

'On trial also is the Nigerian nation, its present rulers and all those who assist them. I am not one of those who shy away from protesting injustice and oppression, arguing that they are expected of a military regime. The military do not act alone. They are supported by a gaggle of politicians, lawyers, judges, academics and businessmen, all of them hiding under the claim that they are only doing their duty, men and women too afraid to wash their pants of their urine. We all stand on trial, my lord, for by our actions we have denigrated our country and jeopardised the future of our children. As we subscribe to the subnormal and accept double standards, as we lie and cheat openly, as we protect injustice and oppression, we empty our classrooms, degrade our hospitals, and make ourselves the slaves of those who subscribe to higher standards, who pursue the truth, and honour justice, freedom and hard work...

'...I predict that a denouement of the riddle of the Niger delta will soon come. The agenda is being set at this trial. Whether the peaceful ways I have favoured will prevail depends on what the oppressor decides, what signals it sends out to the waiting public.

'In my innocence of the false charges I face here, in my utter conviction, I call upon the Ogoni people, the peoples of the Niger delta, and the oppressed ethnic minorities of Nigeria to stand up now and fight fearlessly and peacefully for their rights. History is on their side, God is on their side. For the Holy Quran says in Sura 42, verse 41: "All those who fight when oppressed incur no guilt, but Allah shall punish the oppressor."

'Come the day.' ❑

Ken Saro-Wiwa
Port Harcourt, 1 September 1995

INDEX INDEX

A censorship chronicle incorporating information from Agence France-Presse (AFP), the American Association for the Advancement of Science Human Rights Action Network (AAASHRAN), Amnesty International (AI), Article 19 (A19), the BBC Monitoring Service Summary of World Broadcasts (SWB), the Committee to Protect Journalists (CPJ), the Canadian Committee to Protect Journalists (CCPJ), the Inter-American Press Association (IAPA), the International Federation of Journalists (IFJ/FIP), Human Rights Watch (HRW), the Media Institute of Southern Africa (MISA), International PEN (PEN), Open Media Research Institute Daily Digest (OMRI), Reporters Sans Frontières (RSF) and other sources

ALBANIA

Police and National Intelligence Service officers detained three Socialist Party members in Sarande on 10 September for distributing 'anti-national and anti-constitutional' leaflets. Sulejman Rahman Mekollari, Dilaver Ibrahim Dauti and Lirim Servet Veliu reportedly have long-standing ties with the former Communist regime. (SWB)

A 'genocide and Communist crime' law passed by Parliament on 23 September will bar many ex-Communists from holding public office until 2002. At least seven senior members of the Socialist Party will be affected, as will Social Democratic Party chairman Skender Gjinushi. Senior Socialist politician Gramoz Ruci may have to leave politics as he served as interior minister for two months before March 1991. Opposition leaders are to petition the Council of Europe over some parts of the law. (OMRI, Reuter)

ALGERIA

In protest at the continuing murders of journalists in the civil war, 10 national newspapers withheld publication for three days from 11 September. Omar Ouartilan, editor-in-chief of the Arabic-language daily *al-Khabar*, was shot and killed by an unknown assassin on 3 October as he left his home to go to work. On 16 October Saida Djebaili, journalist for *al-Hayat*, and her driver were shot dead while driving in the centre of Algiers. And Abdelwahab Sadaoui, commercial director of *al-Chaab*, was killed after being abducted from his family's home in Chlef. (Reuter, CPJ, IFJ, *Guardian*)

Recent publication: *Violence: a UNESCO Notebook* (UNESCO, August 1995, 72pp)

ANGOLA

Angolan journalists who fled to Portugal after attacks and threats at home have complained to the Portuguese and Angolan governments about the presence in Lisbon of two officers of the Angolan State Security Ministry. Angolan government sources say that the Ministry has been disbanded, but the journalists believe that the intelligence officers pose a threat to their safety. A spokesman for Angola's President dos Santos said: 'Matters like that [the harassment of journalists] have so little importance that, to be honest with you, they do not deserve any comment on our part.' (MISA)

ARGENTINA

On 12 September the National Criminal Court of Appeals ordered a search of the Buenos Aires daily *La Nación*. The offices were searched for the source and author of a column published in 1993 in which a lawyer was alleged to be practising illegally. On 13 September Judge Angela Braidot upheld the court's decision and ordered a search of the Buenos Aires offices of the daily *Crónica* in relation to the same story. In a separate incident on 13 September, the courts took administrative and editorial control of *El Nuevo Diaro*, a paper in the northern province of Santiago del Estero. A judge took the measure in relation to a defamation suit brought by a lawyer, but revoked it the next day. (IAPA)

AZERBAIJAN

Ayez Ahmadov, editor of the satirical paper *Cheshma*, was sentenced to five years in prison on 19 October for publishing cartoons and jokes that 'insulted the honour and dignity' of President Aliyev (*Index* 3/1995). His co-defendants — journalists Yadigar Memdli, Malik Bayramov and Asker Ahmed, and distributor Mirzaguesein Zeinalov — received sentences of two to three years each. Yamen Abbasov, who works for the Guyesh printing house which publishes the paper, received a two-year suspended sentence. (CPJ, RSF)

BAHRAIN

Pro-democracy activist Sheikh Abd al-Amir Mansur al-Jamri (*Index* 3/1995, 4/1995) was released from detention on 25 September. He had been held without charge or trial in the town of Safira since 15 April. (PEN)

Recent publication: *A Human Rights Crisis* (AI, September 1995, 54pp)

BELARUS

The state printing house Belaruski Dom Petchati cancelled its contract with the opposition paper *Narodnaya Volia* (Will of the People) on 10 October, apparently for an unspecified breach of the press law. The paper is edited by Iosif Seredich, who was sacked as editor of the parliamentary paper *Narodnaya Gazeta* in March in connection with the Antonchyk affair (*Index* 3/1995). On 11 October the Gomel printing house wrote to two further papers — the business journal *Belaruskaya Delovaya Gazeta* and *Imia* (The Name) — to say that it could no longer print them 'owing to needed

repairs'. Both papers had switched to Gomel from the state printing house in the wake of the Antonchyk affair. (RSF)

BOSNIA-HERCEGOVINA

Journalists Munire Acim, of the Turkish daily *Hurriyet* and Alija Kocak, of the Anatolia News Agency, were detained by Bosnian Serb troops at the Sierra 4 checkpoint in Kasindolska on 7 October. It was reported that Bosnian Serb authorities wished to exchange them for two Bosnian Serb television reporters, Sasa Kolevski and Goran Pejcinovic, detained by the Bosnian army on 23 September. On 19 October, however, it was revealed that Kolevski and Pejcinovic had been killed, either while in custody or during fighting near Tuzla. Their bodies were released in exchange for the Acim and Kocak on 21 October. (Reuter, RSF, IFJ, CPJ)

The Sarajevo Serb poet and novelist Vladimir Srebov (*Index* 4/1995) was among a group of prisoners released by Bosnian Serbs on 12 October. He says he was tortured in prison. (OMRI)

UNESCO has announced plans to help Bosnia rebuild its education system when peace is restored. Initial funding for the programme will be between $US60 and 100 million. (Reuter)

Recent publications: *The Missing of Srebrenica* (AI, September 1995, 10pp);

Destination Unknown: Disappeared in Former Yugoslavia (AI, October 1995, 10pp); *The Fall of Srebrenica: War Crimes and the Failure of UN Peacekeeping* (HRW/Helsinki, October 1995, 58pp)

BOTSWANA

In September the *Botswana Guardian* settled out of court in a criminal defamation case brought by Quill Hermans, the governor of the central bank. Hermans sued the paper over a 1993 article alleging that he had mismanaged the bank. The *Guardian* paid 30,000 Botswana pula (US$10,700) plus a further 250,000 pula (US$89,000) for refusing to name their source. (MISA)

BRAZIL

Investigations into police action to evict squatter peasant families from the Santa Elina estate in Corumbiara, Rondônia, on 9 August, have confirmed that police were responsible for gross human rights violations, including extrajudicial executions (*Index* 5/1995). Eleven squatters remain unaccounted for and fears for their safety have been heightened by the discovery on 23 August of the body of Sergio Rodríguez Gomes two weeks after he was taken away by the military police. (AI)

Reinaldo Coutinho da Silva, owner of the weekly *Cachoeiras Jornal* in the village of Cachoeiras de Macac, Rio de Janeiro state, was shot dead on 29 August while driving through the neighbouring town of São Goncalo. Police believe he was killed because of articles he had published about official corruption. (IAPA)

In September the murders were reported of Zaqueu de Oliveira, editor of the newspaper *Gazeta de Barroso* in Minas Gerais state, who was shot and killed on 21 March, allegedly by José Carlos de Souza after a dispute over articles the journalist had written about de Souza's wife; and Aristeu Guida da Silva, owner of the paper *A Gazeta de São Fidelis* in São Fidelis, northwest of Rio de Janeiro, who was shot dead on 12 May by two men driving motorbikes. Da Silva had been receiving death threats for articles accusing the president of the local municipal council of corruption. The case remains unsolved. (CPJ)

On 6 October two *Jornal do Brasilia* journalists were threatened by guards at the federal government building (Palacio do Planalto). Reporter Fabiana Santos, photographer Tony Winston and their driver, Vincente de Paulo Silva, were forced at gunpoint to lie on the ground, beaten and threatened with death. They were investigating reports of homeless people occupying government property. (RSF)

An evangelical preacher is under investigation by a Rio judge and may be charged for punching and kicking an effigy of Our Lady of Aparecida, Brazil's patron saint, on a television programme on 12

October, the saint's feast day. (Reuter)

BULGARIA

On 13 September the Constitutional Court overruled parts of the local election law which forbids journalists in state media from expressing opinions in their reporting of local elections taking place in late October. (*Index* 5/1995). (OMRI)

The Constitutional Court ruled on 19 September that Parliament may no longer approve the regulations, structures, financing, programming and management boards of state radio, television and the Bulgarian News Agency (BTA). Under the 1991 'provisional statute', a parliamentary committee controls state media bodies, pending the adoption of a new media law. On 16 October the leader of the Union of Democratic Forces (SDS) called for the suspension and prosecution of national television director Ivan Granitski (*Index* 4/1995, 5/1995) for exceeding his authority by refusing to broadcast an SDS declaration and an SDS statement protesting the 'violation of the provisional statute of the state-run media'. The statute obliges national media to reflect all political views and gives political parties the right to express their views on radio and television. (OMRI)

BURMA

On 27 September Ko Ye Htut, a Rangoon student, was arrested for 'disseminating fab-

ricated news' to foreign news organisations. He is accused of sending information criticising the ruling State Law and Order Restoration Council (SLORC) to the Bangkok-based Burma Information Group (BIG), to members of his family in Canada, and to the Democratic Voice of Burma (DVB) radio station, based in Oslo. The BIG has stated that Ko Ye Htut only sent them newspapers and magazines published by the SLORC, and the DVB has denied having any contact with the student. (HRW, Reuter, SWB)

On 11 October opposition leader Aung San Suu Kyi was reappointed general secretary of the National League for Democracy, the party she helped found seven years ago. Two other senior party members released from prison in March, Tin Oo and Kyi Maung, were appointed vice-chairmen. (Reuter)

Recent publication: *Conditions in Prisons and Labour Camps* (AI, September 1995, 7pp)

CAMBODIA

Six men charged with incitement on August 14 for distributing leaflets critical of the government (*Index* 5/1995, p81) were released from prison on 18 September, after the charges were dropped. On August 28 King Sihanouk had written to the prime ministers asking that they be given an amnesty.

It was reported on 2 October that the Thai-owned

International Broadcasting Corporation (IBC), Cambodia's only independent television station, is to be taken over jointly by the Ministry of Defence and a new Thai company. Co-defence minister Tea Bahn said: 'We will use the channel to broadcast military news, training and exercises.' (Human Rights Task Force)

On 6 October the Court of Appeal upheld the conviction of Chan Rotana (*Index* 2/1995, 5/1995), editor of *Samleng Yuvachan Khmer* (Voice of Khmer Youth). The court also agreed to a prosecution request to change the charge from article 62 (misinformation) to article 63 (defamation). Rotana's original sentence, of a year in prison and a 5 million riel (US$2,000) fine, was upheld, even though defamation carries a lesser penalty than misinformation. (Reuter, Human Rights Task Force)

On 13 October the Court of Appeal also upheld the conviction for defamation of Thun Bun Ly, editor of *Odum K'tek Khmer* (Khmer Ideal) (*Index* 5/1995). He was ordered to pay a fine of 5 million riel (US$2,000) or be imprisoned for one month. The newspaper was ordered to shut in two months. The charge stemmed from a letter to the editor on 30 October 1994, which referred to the prime ministers as 'barking'. Thun Bun Ly said he would have printed a retraction had the government asked for one. (Reuter, Human Rights Task Force)

Cambodia's two prime ministers have asked a court to press criminal disinformation charges against Michael Hayes, publisher of the English-language *Phnom Penh Post* (*Index* 5/1995, p81). Hayes has received no formal notification of the charges and First Prime Minister Prince Norodom Ranariddh has said he does not wish to close the paper down. (Reuter, *International Herald Tribune*)

Three truck-loads of men armed with poles and axes broke into the offices of the paper *Serei Pheap Thmey* (New Liberty News) on 23 October. They ransacked the offices, destroyed equipment and injured an office worker, Dour Bunma. Police who arrived at the scene while the attack was in progress reportedly did nothing to intervene. (Human Rights Task Force)

Recent publication: *The War Against Free Speech* (HRW/Asia, September 1995, 15pp); *Impunity in Kampot Province* (AI, October 1995, 10pp)

CANADA

In September the Supreme Court ruled that the Tobacco Products Control Act (1988), which bans most forms of cigarette advertising and promotion, violates tobacco companies' constitutional right to freedom of expression. (*Financial Times*)

Stéphane Beaudoin, a cameraman with CHOT television in Hull, Québec, was jailed for contempt of court on 19 September after refusing to name a source before a preliminary hearing in an assault case brought against a Hull police officer. He was freed on 22 September after the defence lawyer agreed to retract his question to Beaudoin, freeing him from the obligation to reveal the source. (CCPJ)

CHILE

Protests that marked the 22nd anniversary of the military coup that toppled President Allende erupted into violence on 11 September. Police used tear gas and water cannons to disperse thousands of protesters in central Santiago and outside the cemetery where Allende is buried. Officials said the protests were stronger than usual owing to recent tensions between the military and the civilian government. (Reuter)

CHINA

Xin Hong, who had been held for eight months for 'leaking state secrets' to her son, exiled police official Gao Peiqi, was released from detention in May. (AI)

Dissidents and their relatives were subject to police surveillance and detention over the period of the UN World Conference on Women in Beijing. Qi Zhiyong, a Beijing resident, was detained without warrant on 28 August. Xu Shuiliang was served a 15-day detention order on 5 September in Nanjing. Wang Zhihong, wife of Chen Ziming (*Index*

4/1995), was ordered to move to the jail where her husband is imprisoned on 29 August, and stayed there for about a month. Yan Huili, wife of Zhang Xianliang, was also moved from her home in Shanghai and sent to her husband's labour camp. During the conference Wang Lingyun (mother of dissident Wang Dan) and Zhu Hailan were kept under 24-hour surveillance and told to report their telephone conversations to police. Huang Xiang and his wife Zhang Ling were not allowed to go to Beijing and Jiang Qisheng was called in for questioning daily. (AI)

Liu Gang, released from prison in June, was sentenced to 15 days' detention in Liaoyuan for breaching parole conditions. The 13 conditions imposed on Liu included a requirement to report his 'thoughts and activities' to the police every week. Liu was released after 10 days and since then he and his family have been under police surveillance. Christian activists Gao Feng and Liu Fenggang were detained in Beijing in early August in connection with the Liu case - a draft appeal on behalf of the dissident was found at Gao Feng's home and confiscated. (AI)

At the NGO forum running alongside the UN conference, Tibetan delegates were subject to especially heavy surveillance. They were routinely followed and their movements and exchanges were filmed by plainclothes police. NGO video footage of interviews with Tibetan women was

confiscated by staff at the Shan Hu Hotel. At a workshop organised by Tibetan women, police attempted to seize a video on forced abortions and sterilisations in Tibet, but lost the tape after a scuffle with members of the audience. The forum's official newspaper - Forum '95 - disappeared for a day in early September after it criticised the arrangements at the forum and carried material from an organisation that had not been granted a licence to publish. Chinese-language materials on the global lesbian movement were seized from the lesbian tent at the forum by Chinese authorities (Guardian, Independent, Sunday Times)

Private businessmen were prohibited from joining the Communist Party in mid-September. In response to criticism that this could hamper careers, Beijing suggested that collective enterprises could still be considered for membership. Individual businessmen who do not hire staff are still eligible. (Reuter)

Film director Zhang Yimou was reportedly advised by Beijing officials at the end of September not to attend the New York film festival, where his Shanghai Triad was to be the opening film. China had complained about the inclusion of a US-made documentary, The Gate of Heavenly Peace, about the Tiananmen Square massacre of 1989. A year ago, Zhang was banned from working on Shanghai Triad, from working with foreign film companies for five years and from attending any

international film festivals, after the unauthorised screening of his film To Live at the 1994 Cannes film festival, where it won two awards. The sanctions against him were reversed, however, after he submitted a 'self-criticism' about sending the film to Cannes without permission, saying that the fact he had not gone to Cannes himself was 'an expression of his attitude and of his respect for the examination departments' and that he had no desire to undermine 'the image of the country' (see also p73). (International Herald Tribune, Reuter, Lien Ho Pao, Ming Pao)

The first Sundance film festival to be held in China took place between 5 and 12 October. The event was a showcase for US and Chinese independent films, all of which were allowed to be screened uncut. However, some Chinese film-makers voiced concern that if restrictions on the number of foreign films China imports each year are lifted, it could seriously threaten the local film industry. (Reuter)

Chen Ziming (see above) went on hunger strike on 13 October at Beijing No 2 prison in protest at his continued imprisonment, the confiscation of his property, the freezing of his bank account, and the authorities' refusal to allow him medical attention: he is suffering from cancer. On 22 October Chen's wife, Wang Zhihong, was detained by police after family members staged a sit-in at a Beijing park. Police also prevented several foreign journalists from covering the protest. (Reuter, SWB, *South China Morning Post*)

At least 10 leading signatories of pro-democracy petitions circulated in May (*Index* 4/1995) remain in detention but only one, Deng Huanwu, has been charged and tried. The detainees include Liu Xiaobo, Wang Dan, and Liu Nianchun. (AI)

Recent publications: *Crackdown on Tibetan Dissent Continues* (AI, September 1995, 6pp); *Update on Dissidents Detained Around 4 June 1995* (AI, September 1995, 7pp)

COLOMBIA

Hernando Valencia Villa, who resigned in August as deputy attorney-general in charge of human rights, flew to Madrid on 1 September, where he was granted political asylum. He had received death threats after calling for the dismissal of General Alvaro Velandia, who is linked to the murder in 1987 of M-19 militant Erika Bautista. On 11 September President Samper ordered Velandia to be dismissed, the first time a military general has been removed for human rights violations. (Reuter)

On 20 September unidentified gunmen killed at least 24 people and injured another five in a massacre outside the town of Apartado, in the region of Uraba. Banana workers, most of them members of the local

Hope, Peace and Freedom party, were forced from a bus which had been stopped by a makeshift roadblock and then shot. President Samper immediately introduced emergency measures in the area, allowing police to conduct arrests, summary searches and seizures without warrants. On 3 October another similar attack in Uraba left two banana plantation workers dead. (Reuter)

On 24 September Jesús Emilio and Luis Tiberio Galvis Barrera, members of the Community Action Movement of Aguachica, (MACA), were stopped by a heavily armed group of men, some wearing the insignia of the Counter-Insurgency Task Force, while travelling by road from the village of Yeura, department of Cesar. They were later found tortured and beheaded. Later the same day an armed group, believed to be the same one that abducted the Galvis brothers, ransacked the communal shop in the village of La Morena, municipality of Aguachica, and reportedly killed the local police inspector, Emelda Ruiz. (AI)

Antonio José Cancino, President Samper's lawyer, was attacked and wounded on 27 September on his way to his office in Bogotá. One Administrative Department of Security (DAS) agent was killed and two members of the bodyguard corps injured in the attack, which followed death threats against the lawyer who is defending Samper against charges that

his presidential campaign was funded by drug cartels (*Index* 5/1995). (Reuter)

A new paramilitary organisation called the Henry Pérez Group issued a letter in early October, threatening the lives of 23 union leaders and politicians in Barrancabermeja who it claims are linked to various left-wing insurgent groups. (SWB)

Recent publication: *Women in Colombia — Breaking the Silence* (AI, September 1995, 18pp)

COTE D'IVOIRE

On 20 September the government issued a decree banning 'all marches and sit-ins' for a three-month period. The ban comes at the beginning of the presidential election campaign, which is to be followed by legislative and municipal elections at the end of this year. Access for opposition political parties to the national media has also been severely restricted. (A19)

The offices of the *Nouvel Horizon* newspaper group were destroyed by fire on the evening of 16-17 October. The fire, which appears to have been set deliberately, followed violent demonstrations on 16 October by opponents of the government calling for a boycott of the presidential election. (RSF)

COSTA RICA

On 4 August the body of David Maradiaga, head of communications and campaigns for the Costa Rican Ecology Association (AECO-Friends of the Earth), was discovered in the city morgue nearly three weeks after he disappeared. The authorities claimed that Maradiaga had been there since 14 July. Maradiaga had been working on a campaign against the Canadian mining company Placer Dome, currently negotiating exploration rights over a rich, tropical forest zone with the governments of Costa Rica and Nicaragua. Maradiaga's death adds to the series of suspicious deaths of Costa Rican environmentalists. On 7 December 1994 a fire in the home of two AECO members, Oscar Fallas and Maria del Mar Cordero, killed them and their director, Jaime Bustamant. (*Latinamerica Press*)

On 25 August Andres Borrasse Sanaou, the publisher of *La Prensa Libre*, was ordered to pay 5.6 million Colóns (US$5,600) compensation in a case brought by Carlos Campos of the Union of Small Atlantic Flower Growers. Campos objected to claims in the paper that the union was undergoing militarisation. Borrasse has said he will appeal. (IAPA)

CROATIA

A new election law, passed in September, reduces the number of seats in Parliament from 138 to 127, of which only 28 will be elected by direct district vote and 12 will be elected by party lists among registered voters working abroad. The threshold for entry to Parliament is raised

from 3 per cent to 5 per cent of the total vote. The number of seats reserved for the Serbian minority is reduced and the Bosnian Muslim minority — Croatia's second largest ethnic minority — has no guaranteed representation at all. Opponents of the law say it favours the ruling Croatian Democratic Community (HDZ). (OMRI)

On 8 October an election coalition of five opposition parties protested Croatian Television's decision to treat them as a single entity and not five separate parties, thus limiting them to only one block of free airtime. The opposition Croatian Social Liberal Party also protested a television ban on its promotional videos, which have also been banned by the company that

Farkhad Kerimov
1948 - 1995

The Trustees and Committee of the **Rory Peck Award** congratulate the family, friends and colleagues of Farkhad Kerimov, winner of this year's Freelance Television Cameramen's Award for his outstanding report on the Russian assault on Grozny, Chechenya.

Information about the 1996 Award and the **Rory Peck Trust** for the dependants of Freelance Cameramen and Women can be obtained from: The Secretary, The Rory Peck Award, York Road Mews, Healaugh, Tadcaster, N Yorkshire, LS24 8DD, UK. Tel: +44 1937 835 933 or Fax +44 1937 833 743 owns most of the country's cinemas. Unbalanced news coverage and curbs on television access have been criticised by observers from the Washington-based National Democratic Institute, which has expressed concern over the fairness of the elections. (OMRI, Reuter)

Radovan Jovic, a Serbian former judge in Krajina and member of the independent intellectuals' organisation Belgrade Circle, was arrested in Tucipe on 24 October along with 14 others and charged with espionage. He was on his way home after attending the Fourth Helsinki Citizens' Assembly in Tuzla. (HCA)

CUBA

Independent journalists Rafael Solano and Yndamiro Restano (*Index* 4/1995) were interrogated by state security officials in Havana on 15 September. Their families were warned that the state could not take responsibility for any future violent action against them because of their 'illegal activities'. (CPJ)

On 19 September the new Independent Press Bureau of Cuba (BPIC) issued its first press release. Several journalists working for the Bureau, run by Yndamiro Restano, have been warned by police that they must find work with a state organisation or face prosecution for 'dangerousness'. On 3 October Roxana Valdivia, BPIC's Camagüey correspondent, was detained by state security agents for 20

hours. Her equipment and documents were confiscated and she was ordered to return to Camagüey and to abandon her professional duties in Havana. On 4 October Maria de los Angeles Gutiérrez, the Bureau's accountant, was detained by security forces for several hours and told to find another job. On 7 October BPIC journalist Olance Nogueras was given a similar warning by police in Cienfuegos. On 10 October Héctor Peraza Linares was picked up by police in Quiricam and threatened with a charge of 'vagrancy'. On 20 October, Nogueras was detained but released two days later, only to be arrested again on 25 October after police surrounded BPIC's office in Havana. (AI, RSF, CPJ, BPIC)

Recent publication: *Improvements Without Reform* (HRW/Americas, October 1995, 34pp)

EGYPT

Youssef Chahine's popular film *al-Muhajer* (The Emigrant) (*Index* 1/1995, 2/1995, 3/1995) was banned for the second time on 31 August on the grounds that it contravenes Islamic rulings about depiction of prophets. The film was first banned in November 1994 after a case was brought against it by an Islamist lawyer. Chahine successfully appealed against the ban in March but a counter-appeal was subsequently filed. (Reuter)

Wahid Hamed and Sharif

Arafa, producer and director of the film *Birds of Darkness*, appeared in a Cairo court on 8 October at the start of a suit brought by a lawyer, Mahmoud Riyad, who accuses them of insulting the legal profession in the film. It depicts corruption among lawyers and government officials. The case was adjourned until 19 November. (Reuter)

Recent publication: *Deaths in Custody* (AI, October 1995, 10pp)

EL SALVADOR

A draft bill before Congress would allow only the attorney-general's office to release information to the press about legal cases. The bill would make it a criminal offence for any other official — such as a judge or police officer — to issue such information, and for any media outlet to publish it. It is feared that the measure could be used to withhold information pertaining to cases of government corruption. (IAPA)

EUROPEAN UNION

On 5 October the EU Social Affairs Council called on European publishers, broadcasters and advertisers to end sexual stereotyping in the media. A non-binding resolution adopted by the Council said that 'advertising and the media can play an important role in changing attitudes in society by reflecting the diversity of the roles and potential of women and men'; that stereotypes can harm mental and physical health; and that the media must find new ways to portray men and women. The resolution was criticised by the European Newspaper Publishers' Association for 'introducing censorship'. (Reuter)

FRANCE

The prime minister, Alain Juppé, ordered his staff to stop buying the satirical weekly *Le Canard Enchaîné*, which recently published highly damaging allegations that he had used his influence to reduce the rent on his son's Paris apartment. The weekly responded on 4 October by publishing a subscription coupon on its front page, made out in Juppé's name. 'Since we are anxious that the prime minister of France should be as well informed as possible, our journal has decided to give him a free subscription,' the paper declared. (*Times*)

GAMBIA

On 27 September Pap Saine, co-editor of the *Point* newspaper and two of his reporters, Brima Ernest and Alieu Badara Sowe, were acquitted after a six-month trial of 'disseminating false news to cause fear and alarm to the public' in relation to an article published on 30 March (*Index* 3/1995). The next day Pap Saine's passport was seized by immigration officials, though it was returned the next day. Brima Ernest was forced to go into hiding as immigration officials searched for him with the aim of deporting him to Sierra Leone. He has since

fled the country and is living in exile. (PEN, *Daily Observer*, SWB)

GERMANY

Thirty thousand Bavarians demonstrated in Munich on 23 September against the Constitutional Court's ban against displaying crucifixes in Bavarian classrooms (*Index* 5/1995). Legal officials say that the protest, held under the motto 'The Cross Stays - Yesterday, Today and Tomorrow', threatens the authority of the Federal Constitutional Court, and accuse conservative politicians of whipping up the protests. (*International Herald Tribune*, Reuter)

GHANA

In October the government urged journalists not to use abusive language when writing about the government. 'They should criticise the government, tear its policies apart and take it to task, but that should be done decently,' an official statement said. (*West Africa*)

GUATEMALA

Three Presbyterian church leaders received death threats from the Avenging Jaguar death squad on 8 August, in connection with their campaign to bring to justice the killer of Manuel Saquic, a Presbyterian human rights worker murdered in June. (*Latinamerica Press*)

Lisbeth Valenzuela Bustamante and Luis Samayoa

Barrera, first-year law students at the San Carlos University in Guatemala City, have been subjected to threats and surveillance since 17 August. Samayoa participated in a protest by the Association of University Students (AEU) against the lack of investigation into the extrajudicial murder of fellow student Mario Alioto López in November 1994. (AI)

On 23 August the Appeals Court decided to proceed with charges of forced recruitment in the Department of Huehuetenango against army general Luis Miranda Trejo. (*Human Rights Bulletin*)

The National Agrarian Co-ordinating Commission, representing landowners, backed by CACIF, Guatemala's largest private-sector organisation, filed legal charges against the government's highest peace negotiator, Héctor Rosada, on 18 October, accusing him of crimes ranging from misuse of power to illicit association with illegal groups.

GUINEA

On 28 September Souleymane Diallo, managing editor of *Le Lynx*, was given a three-month suspended sentence for offending President Conte by publishing a cartoon in the 14 August edition of the paper. He was also fined 2.5 million Guinean francs (US$5,100). (RSF)

HAITI

On 5 September members of

popular organisations attended the trial of Legalier Louis, one of those accused of the 1993 murder of radio technician Jean Claude Dimache. The judge ruled that he would have to release Louis because only 29 of the 30 jury members had turned up. Demonstrators inside and outside the courtroom prevented the release by nailing the court's doors shut. (*Haiti Info*)

HONDURAS

On 17 October Judge Roy Medina ordered the arrest of Colonel Alexander Hernández and retired officers Major Manuel de Jesús Trejo and Captain Billy Joya on charges of illegal detention and attempted murder of students 13 years ago. This is the first time a court has ordered the arrest of military officers. The officers had refused previous orders to testify in court. Their defence lawyers claimed that they are protected by a 1991 amnesty law. (AI)

INDIA

Kashmiri newspapers went on strike for eight days from 20 September to protest demands by two rival factions of the Jammu and Kashmir Liberation Front (JKLF) that their views be given prominence on news pages. Sheikh Mushtaq, former Srinagar bureau chief of the *Daily Excelsior*, said: 'Journalists insist on objectivity; either publish both sides or not at all.' (Reuter)

Recent publications: *The Delhi Massacre: an Example of*

Malicious Government and *Human Rights in Bihar* (both Khalsa Human Rights, 13pp and 12pp); *Deaths in Custody 1994* (AI, 29pp)

INDONESIA

The award to Pramoedya Ananta Toer (*Index* 5/1981, 4/1986, 10/1989, 3/1990, 3/1995) of the Magsaysay Prize for Literature in August has provoked differing reactions in Indonesia. Twenty-six people from the arts and literature world issued a statement criticising the award, and former winner Mochtar Lubis handed back his own award, saying Pramoedya 'had done very bad things against Indonesian writers and artists when the Communist Party was in power'. In response, 154 people signed an open letter supporting Pramoedya, noting that his writings and statements are banned. Pramoedya was barred from travelling to Manila to accept the award because he is a former political prisoner. (*Far Eastern Economic Review*, Tapol)

On 25 September the memoirs of former cabinet minister Oei Tjoe Tat were banned by the attorney-general. The memoirs were edited by Pramoedya Ananta Toer. (*Far Eastern Economic Review*)

On 11 September Tri Agus Susanto (*Index* 3/1995), editor-in-chief of *Kabar dari Pijar* (News from Pijar), was found guilty of insulting the government and sentenced to two years' imprisonment. (Tapol, RSF)

Controversial soothsayer Permadi Satrio Wiwoho was sentenced to seven months in jail for blasphemy on 12 September. He was accused of making a speech in which he described the Prophet Mohammed as a 'dictator', but Permadi claims a tape of his speech, which was produced as evidence in court, was doctored. (Tapol, *Jakarta Post*)

On 15 September 70 members of the Assembly for Safeguarding People's Sovereignty called for Information Minister Harmoko to be tried for insulting Islam. The call arose from a pun that Harmoko allegedly made with a verse of the Quran while officiating at a puppet show in Java in September. (SWB)

On 8 October the Alliance of Independent Journalists (AJI) held its first conference since it was set up in August 1994. At the meeting members listened to recorded messages from imprisoned AJI members Ahmad Taufik, Eko Maryadi and Danang Wardaya. (*Index* 4/1995, 5/1995). (AJI)

Recent publication: *Surveillance and Suppression: The Legacy of the 1965 Coup in Indonesia* (A19, 1995, 16pp)

IRAN

A bride was sentenced to 85 lashes by an Islamic court in early September for dancing with men at her wedding. Her father and 127 guests were also sentenced to flogging or fined. (Reuter)

The parliamentary Islamic Culture and Guidance Committee met officials from the Arts Council and the Islamic Guidance Ministry in mid-September to decide whether to lift a ban, imposed in February, on the film *Snowman.* The film, made by Iranian director Davoud Mir-Baqeri, depicts the corrupting influence of western culture on a young Muslim. The officials feared that the film itself might have a corrupting effect on the audience, and have so far been unable to come to a decision on the ban. (*Salam*)

Mohammad Javad Larijani, vice-chairman of the Parliamentary Foreign Affairs Committee, said in October that the *fatwa* against British author Salman Rushdie is an Islamic ruling that is accepted by all Muslims, but that the Iranian government respects international law and has no desire to endanger the life of any civilian. He suggested that relations between Iran and the EU would improve if European governments stopped supporting Rushdie and 'promoting his crime against Islam'. (*Iran News*)

The Mashad-based daily *Tous* was shut down by the authorities on 19 October until further notice for violating the defamation laws. The paper's editor said he was unaware of any complaints against it. (Reuter)

On 2 October the Censorship of Publications Board decided to lift a ban on *Playboy* maga-zine, which has been in effect for 36 years (*Index* 4/1995). (*Guardian*)

ISRAEL & OCCUPIED TERRITORIES

Maureen Meehan, a journalist with US National Public Radio, was arrested by Israeli police while covering a demonstration outside Orient House, the PLO building in East Jerusalem that was recently ordered closed by Israeli authorities. Israeli police claimed she had kicked a police officer. Meehan's husband said she had been arrested to prevent her report-ing on the breakup of the demonstration by police. (Reuter)

Birzeit University in the West Bank launched its 'Academic Freedom First' campaign in September, calling for fairer treatment of Gazan students studying in Israeli and West Bank universities. Gazan stu-dents currently require four different permits in order to study outside Gaza and are therefore vulnerable to the frequent blanket cancellations of permits that leave them unable to travel to and from college freely. Birzeit is calling for a single special academic permit for its 350 Gazan stu-dents which would guarantee access during academic terms. (*Jerusalem Times*)

Samir Hamatou, a freelance journalist based in Gaza who works for *Ma'ariv* and *al Hayah al Jadida*, was sentenced to five months in prison on 27 September for 'security offences'. He was freed on 10 October as part of the release of detainees mandated by the second part of the Oslo accords. (Palestinian Media Monitoring Centre)

The government partially lift-ed restrictions on the access of Palestinian journalists to Israel and East Jerusalem on 17 October (*Index* 2/1995). Those above the age of 30 are now allowed to travel to their Jerusalem offices, as long as they do not use private trans-port. (Palestinian Media Monitoring Centre)

The prime minister, Yitzhak Rabin, has rejected calls for an investigation into allegations that Israeli soldiers killed Egyptian prisoners during wars with its neighbours. The allegations surfaced when a retired brigadier-general con-fessed to executing 49 prison-ers during the 1956 Suez war, and escalated when a journal-ist, Gabriel Brun, claimed to have witnessed executions at El Arish airbase in the Sinai desert while serving in the 1967 Six Day War. Egypt is demanding a full inquiry, and Israeli communications minis-ter Shulamit Aloni has also said that the issue must be dealt with openly. (*Independent*)

Recent publications: *Incidents of Death and Injury Resulting from Exploding Munitions Remnants* (B'Tselem, July 1995, 20pp); *Intifada-Related Head Injuries: a Report by the Association of Israeli-Palestinian Physicians for Human Rights* (PHR, PO Box 10235, Tel Aviv 61101, tel +00 972 3 5664526, July 1995, 42pp);

Death by Shaking: the Case of 'Abd al-Samad Harizat (AI, October 1995, 17pp)

ITALY

Pasolini, an Italian Crime, a film by Marco Tullio Giordana, has reopened the public debate on the brutal murder of film director and poet Pier Paolo Pasolini in 1975. The film shows that there was substantial forensic evidence to suggest that Pino Pelosi, who was sentenced to nine years in prison for the murder, had at least one accomplice — a fact that was ignored during Pelosi's trials. Pasolini was an outspoken critic of Italy's corrupt political establishment of the 1970s, and his work was frequently censored. Giordana's film, which mixes modern reconstruction with historical footage, hints that powerful groups blocked a proper investigation into the murder. (Reuter)

JAPAN

The government is considering invoking the controversial 1952 Subversive Activities Prevention Act in order to ban the Aum Shinrikyo sect, which has been accused of carrying out nerve-gas attacks in Matsumoto and Tokyo. Other measures currently under debate include revisions to the religious corporations law, to allow the government greater freedom to check the accounts and documents of religious groups. Many religious groups, and the Shinshinto opposition party, oppose the amendments and

argue that they would infringe religious freedom and the principle of the separation of church and state. (*International Herald Tribune*, Reuter)

JORDAN

Salameh Ne'mat, Amman correspondent for the London–based Arabic-language newspaper *al-Hayat*, was jailed for two days on 3 October and then released on bail. He is charged with violating the Press and Publications Law because of an article published on 20 September, alleging that many Jordanian professionals received money from the Iraqi government during the 1990 Gulf War. (CPJ)

KENYA

Koigi wa Wamwere (*Index* 2/1995, p17, and see also above, p164) was sentenced on 2 October to four years in jail and six strokes of the cane, after the capital charge of armed robbery was dropped. Three of the four co-accused were found guilty of simple robbery (although they were not charged with this) and defence lawyers have said they will appeal the verdict. In a letter smuggled to an observer at his trial, wa Wamwere again attacked corruption in the government and judicial system and accused President Moi of using the trial as an excuse to get rid of him before the 1997 elections. His lawyers filed an appeal on 16 October but the High Court adjourned the case until 6 November. (Reuter, MISA, PEN)

Home affairs minister Francis Lotodo told Parliament on 18 October that an average of three prisoners die every day in Kenya's congested prisons. From January to the end of September, 819 inmates died, 291 of whom had not been convicted. In a ceremony to mark the anniversary of his becoming president on 11 October, President Moi ordered the release of 10,898 prisoners, mainly petty offenders with less than six months of their terms to serve. (Reuter)

KYRGYZSTAN

Zamiura Sydykova and Tamara Slashcheva, editor and deputy editor of the paper *Res Publica* (*Index* 5/1995), were freed in August after Parliament passed a general amnesty law as part of a series of national celebrations to mark the 1.000th anniversary of The Manas epic, the world's longest poem. (Glasnost Defence Foundation)

Several journalists were beaten by security forces in Bishkek on 27 August while covering a meeting of the leaders of Turkish-speaking countries. (Glasnost Defence Foundation)

The Human Rights Movement of Kyrgyzstan (HRMK) called for the impeachment of President Akayev on 8 October, for violating the Constitution, misleading Parliament and imposing media censorship. The HRMK said that the country's media monopolies must be broken up and that a new law on freedom of speech must be introduced in order to preserve an independent, critical press. (SWB, *Res Publica*)

LATVIA

Inese Skutane, a reporter for the Baltic News Service, was abducted in Riga on 27 September, by three men who drove her to the waterfront, hit her over the head and forced her to swim in the cold water. The men told Skutane they would not kill her 'until she saw the results of the elections the following weekend'. (CPJ)

LEBANON

In September authorities banned a concert by British heavy metal band Iron Maiden, which was scheduled for October. No official reason was given, but one possibility is that heavy metal music is being blamed for teenage suicides. (*Observer*)

LIBYA

On 28 September the authorities decided to expel all Palestinian residents (estimated to number between 25,000 and 30,000), as well as other foreign residents, including Sudanese and Egyptian migrant workers. Many Palestinians are long-term residents without travel papers or rights of residency elsewhere. Lebanon, Egypt, Jordan and Israel have warned that they will not offer residency to the refugees and Palestinians are unable to travel to Gaza with-

out Israel's permission. Libyan leader Muammar Qaddafi stated that the expulsions are intended to allow Palestinians to 'return' to the autonomous Palestinian areas of Gaza and Jericho but other sources claim that, following recent unrest in Benghazi and central Libya, the authorities see migrants as a threat to national security. (*Middle East International*)

MACEDONIA

Parliament voted on 5 October to change the country's flag as a concession to Greece. A sun with eight broad rays replaces the 16-point star of Vergina (*Index* 5/1995). Parts of Macedonia's Constitution will also be clarified. In return, Greece agreed to lift its blockade of Macedonia. Another contentious issue, Macedonia's name, is to be discussed separately. (OMRI)

On 7 and 8 October several officials of the pro-Bulgarian Internal Macedonia Revolutionary Organisation-Fatherland Party were arrested and party offices were searched, possibly in connection with the attempted assassination of President Kiro Gligorov. The Bulgarian Foreign Ministry expressed concern at press speculation of a Bulgarian connection to the assassination attempt and at 'procedural irregularities' in the arrests. (SWB, OMRI)

MALAYSIA

The information minister announced on 27 September

that the government will launch a new radio station next year to counter 'negative' reports on the country. The minister said that some tourists and investors believed it was unsafe to invest in Malaysia due to people spreading lies about it. (*South China Morning Post*)

On 19 October the prime minister ordered a review of the ban on television programmes featuring people in Chinese historical costumes. The television channel Metrovision was forced to withdraw two costume dramas in October, one Taiwanese and one Chinese, because they contravene the 20-year-old ruling. (SWB, Reuter)

MAURITIUS

On 3 August the death penalty was abolished, bringing the worldwide total of abolitionist countries to 98. (AI)

European ambassadors are using 'quiet diplomacy' to help bring to an end the threats and intimidation against the editor of *L'Indépendant*, Namassiwayam Ramalingum (*Index* 3/1995, 4/1995). Despite being assured by the president of the Muslim Council in Mauritius that there is no *fatwa* against him, Ramalingum is still living in fear of his life. (MISA)

MEXICO

Dozens of members of the Democratic Revolutionary Party (PRD) and their families received death threats in the run-up to the 15 October

REPORTERS SANS FRONTIÈRES

election in the state of Chiapas. On 17 September Artemio Roblero Roblero, a PRD candidate, was murdered outside his home by gunmen believed to be members of the *Guardias Blancas*, employed by local landowners. On 19 September Higinio Sánchez Hernández, a PRD candidate, was shot dead and his brother Apolinar, a PRD member, was seriously wounded. (AI)

MOROCCO

Eight students held in Salé prison began a hunger strike in September to protest against prison conditions and their alleged torture. The eight were arrested in May by Moroccan authorities for taking part in a demonstration supporting the Polisario Front, the Western Saharan independence organisation. Although they were originally sentenced to 20 years in prison, the sentences were commuted by King Hassan to one year. (SWB)

Recent publication: *Human Rights in Morocco* (HRW/Middle East, October 1995, 42pp)

NICARAGUA

On 9 August the national police chief, Fernando Caldera, received a telephone death threat after he announced the arrest of three people suspected of involvement in a series of bomb attacks on 13 Catholic churches since May. On 14 August six more people were arrested. However, on 26 August an explosion shattered the windows of a chapel in Masaya. Days earlier, Cardinal Miguel Obando y Bravo received a phone call telling him that he would be killed in a car bomb. (*Latinamerica Press*)

NIGERIA

It was reported in October that the well-known writer Mohammed Sule has been detained without charge since 9 February. He is apparently being held in connection with a documentary he was attempting to make entitled *Nigeria at the Crossroads*. He has been refused visits from his wife since July, and is said to be suffering from hypertension. (PEN)

The trial of writer and minority rights activist Ken Saro-Wiwa is due to reach its conclusion at the end of October (*Index* 2/1995, 5/1995). In mid-September Saro-Wiwa started a hunger strike in protest at his treatment in detention, raids on his offices in Lagos and Port Harcourt, the continued harassment of the Ogoni people, and the unfairness of his trial. (PEN)

On 18 October Kwara State police arrested four people in connection with the circulation of a leaflet and the publication of an illegal newspaper. A lecturer at the University of Ilorin involved with the publication is reportedly on the run. According to the police, the leaflets were aimed at inciting people against the state government. (SWB)

Recent publications: *Patterns of Abuse of Women's Rights* (Civil Liberties Organisation, 70pp); *The Ogoni Trials and Detentions* (AI, September 1995, 14pp)

NORTH KOREA

Three brothers were forcibly returned from Beijing to Sinuiju, North Korea, in June at the request of the North Korean government, and have since disappeared. They are believed to be vulnerable because their father, Hwang Yong Su, a former prisoner, had given interviews and press conferences criticising the human rights situation in North Korea during a visit to Japan in 1994. (AI)

Recent publication: *What Happened to Cho Ho Pyong and his Family?* (AI, August 1995, 4pp)

PAKISTAN

In August more than 20 employees of the official news agency Associated Press of Pakistan (APP) were dismissed or forced into retirement, following their exposure of alleged financial irregularities in the agency. On 11 October journalists protested outside the national and provincial parliaments, demanding that their colleagues be reinstated.

(Pakistan Press Foundation, Reuter)

Farhan Effendi, Sindh correspondent for *Parcham*, was abducted by paramilitary Rangers on 14 September. He was charged on 15 September with carrying an illegal rifle and remanded in police custody for nine days. Effendi claims he was severely beaten in custody. (Pakistan Press Foundation)

The crisis in Karachi continues: four MQM activists were shot dead while in police custody on 10 October. More than 1,500 people have been killed in violence in Karachi this year. (Human Rights Commission of Pakistan, *Financial Times*)

PALESTINE (GAZA-JERICHO)

The pro-Hamas paper *al-Watan* (*Index* 5/1995) was permitted to reopen on 16 October. (Palestinian Media Monitoring Centre)

PARAGUAY

Lawyer Alberto Alderete has received a series of anonymous death threats at his home in the capital, Asunción, apparently as a result of his representation of peasant farmers killed and injured in clashes with police. The threats followed the presentation in mid-September of a formal criminal complaint against the interior minister, the national police commander and other police officials, accusing them of responsibility for the death of farmer

Pedro Gíminez and injuries to 17 others when members of the Rural and Ecological Police forcibly broke up a demonstration on 7 September. (AI)

PERU

After 33 years in circulation *Oiga* published its last edition on 5 September. The influential weekly political magazine was staunch in its defence of press freedom. Editor-in-chief Francisco Igartua fought frequently against threats from authorities, exile and, finally, closure. (Instituto Prensa y Sociedad)

Four prison guards were dismissed by the National Penitentiary Institute (INPE) on 4 October for assaulting journalists covering the escape of three prisoners from Callao jail in September. (Instituto Prensa y Sociedad)

Congress passed a law on 5 October to extend the use of 'faceless' judges and tribunals until 15 October 1996. Human rights groups expressed concern that several of the journalists detained in Peru were convicted by faceless tribunals and that these tribunals are responsible for many legal abuses. (FIP)

On 10 October journalists at the scene of a crash of a Peruvian Air Force (FAP) plane in Chiclayo were assaulted by FAP officials and soldiers. Rogelio Oblitas Cubas, a photographer for the daily *La República*, was attacked by eight officers and his camera and papers were seized. Jorge Chávez, correspondent for *Caretas*, received the same treatment; and Joyce Machuca, a reporter with Frecuencia Látina television, had her video camera and cassette taken. (Instituto Prensa y Sociedad)

PHILIPPINES

In September the film *Bridges of Madison County* was briefly given an X rating (effectively a ban) by the head of the censorship board, Henrietta Mendez, as a result of a five-second full-frontal shot of a naked Meryl Streep. Her decision was promptly reversed by President Ramos's office and Mendez (who had also banned *Schindler's List*, *The Piano*, and *Belle Epoque*) was sacked. (*Straits Times*, Reuter)

ROMANIA

In September newspapers and opposition politicians issued strong protests at proposed revisions to the Penal Code which would introduce greater restrictions on the media. Revised articles 168 and 236 would allow prison terms of one to five years for 'dissemination of false information' and 'defamation of the nation'. Revised article 206 introduces a maximum penalty of three years in prison for 'defamation through the media', which is greater than the penalty for general defamation. On 16 October Chamber of Deputies Speaker Adrian Nastase met editors to discuss alterations to the draft legislation. (Reuter, OMRI, CPJ, *Adeverul*)

On 6 September the National Audio Council demanded that national television withdraw the BBC-produced series *Up-to-day Week*, made by Romanian journalists on an exchange programme in London, after the 2 September edition alleged that Romania has failed to enforce the fuel embargo on Serbia. The government daily *Vocea Romaniei* accused the BBC of disseminating news 'openly hostile to the government'. (OMRI, *Romanian Times Monitor*, Reuter)

On 12 September the Chamber of Deputies voted to remove the prohibition of homosexual acts from the Penal Code, unless they are committed in public, without consent or involve those under the age of consent (*Index* 1/1995). (OMRI)

The trial on libel charges of *Ziua* journalists Sorin Rosca Stanescu and Tana Ardeleanu began on 18 September (*Index* 5/1995). On 16 October the journalists reportedly launched their own suit against the Interior Ministry's ban on their leaving Romania pending trial. (CCPJ, *Ziua*)

It was reported in October that the prosecutor-general is considering whether to prosecute the ultra-nationalist papers *Politika* and *Romania Mare*, the organ of the Greater Romania Party (PRM), for defamation following their publication of attacks on President Iliescu. One *Romania Mare* pamphlet, written by PRM leader Corneliu Tudor Vadim, reportedly

accused Iliescu of being the protector of 'Impertinent Zionists'. (*Libertatea*, Reuter)

Recent publication: *Update to May 1995 Report* (AI, September 1995, 12pp)

RUSSIAN FEDERATION

Russia: Turkmen poet Shiraly Nurmuradov, who is wanted in Turkmenistan to face charges for drug possession and whom Turkmen authorities were trying to deport from Moscow, was arrested by Russian authorities on 21 September. Nurmuradov's friends believe the charges against him are fabricated. Several days before his arrest, Nurmuradov was given the 1995 Tchkolsky award for writers in exile, which carries a year's residence in Sweden as part of the prize. He is currently receiving treatment in hospital in Moscow, and it is unclear whether he will be able to take up his residency in Sweden. There are serious concerns for his safety if he is returned to Turkmenistan. (PEN)

On 26 September reports that Russian Public Television (ORT) was dropping Alexander Solzhenitsyn's 15-minute social and current affairs programme resulted in protests in Moscow. One of ORT's most controversial programmes, the late-night current affairs show *Versil*, was also axed. *Versil*'s anchorman, Sergei Dorenko, later alleged that senior ORT officials had warned him that the programme's content was unacceptable to the government, a charge denied by the station's director-general. (AFP, *Variety*)

On 3 October the independent newspaper *Nezavisimaya Gazeta* resumed publishing after a four-month suspension (*Index* 4/1995). The paper's editor, Vitaly Tretyakov, who had been forced to use bodyguards at work prior to the suspension, found financing from a local bank to restart the paper. (*Independent*)

Tajik journalist Abdukaum Kaumzod, a reporter for the Moscow-based Tajik newspaper *Charogi Ruz* (*Index* 3/1995), was arrested in Moscow on 8 October. He is wanted in Tajikistan on charges of subversion in connection with his work on the paper. He was released on 10 October, after his case received widespread attention in the Moscow press. (CPJ)

The poet Alina Vitukhnovskaya, who has been detained in the Butirski isolation prison in Moscow since October 1994 on charges of possessing and selling small amounts of drugs, is currently on hunger strike. There are concerns about the legitimacy of the charges against her and international organisations are calling for a thorough and impartial investigation into her case. (PEN)

The case against the publishers of the erotic journal *Yeshcho* (*Index* 2/1995) has been postponed for the fourth time this year. Alexei Kostin, the publisher, has spent a year in prison awaiting the conclusion

of his trial. The article of the code under which he has been charged is no longer applicable under the terms of the new Constitution. (*Guardian*)

Dagestan: Members of a Franco-Russian film company, which included actor Oleg Menshikov and director Sergei Bodrov, were kidnapped and held to ransom by racketeers on 17 October. Dagestani authorities say they are 'powerless' to help and that the remaining crew members must do their best to raise the ransom fee. The crew was working on an adaptation of a Tolstoy story called *The Prisoner of the Caucasus*. (SWB)

RWANDA

UN officials confirmed on 4 October that they are concerned about the fate of a Rwandan journalist for UN radio who has been missing since August. Manasse Mugabo, who works for the UN Assistance Mission in Rwanda, disappeared after going on leave on 15 August. He apparently left his home on 19 August for Uganda and has not been heard of since. (Reuter)

The government appointed a new Supreme Court on 12 October, in the first major step towards rebuilding the justice system destroyed by last year's genocide. The court's members were elected by Parliament. (Reuter)

Recent publication: *L'Impasse? La Liberté de la*

Presse après de la Génocide (RSF, October 1995, 53pp, plus appendices)

SERBIA-MONTENEGRO

Serbia: Miroslav Radulovic, editor-in-chief of the independent paper *Borske Novine*, was sentenced to six months in prison on 12 October, in connection with cartoons published in the paper in August. The cartoons, which depicted nude representations of several Serbian and federal leaders, had earlier appeared in several other papers, without incident. (RSF)

Kosovo: On 12 September the Albanian government protested the settling of Krajina Serb refugees in the Pristina League Memorial Centre and accused the Serbian authorities of provocation and attacking Albanian culture. The memorial is a UNESCO-protected building. (OMRI)

The Prizen district court sentenced 44 Albanian former policemen and local officials to prison terms of between one and six-and-a-half years on 21 September. The accused, on trial since 3 May, were charged with setting up a 'shadow' police force (*Index* 4/1995, 5/1995). (SWB)

SIERRA LEONE

Cherno Ceesay, a journalist with the *Daily Observer*, was arrested on arrival in Sierra Leone in early October, after being expelled from Gambia. He was released on bail on 17 October. His detention in Freetown is believed to be connected to his previous journalistic work in Sierra Leone, where, as editor-in-chief of the newspaper the *Pool*, he was accused by the government of supporting opposition forces in the civil war. His expulsion from Gambia is thought to be related to articles he wrote on alleged police beatings of two Sierra Leoneans. (RSF, CPJ, *Daily Observer*)

Recent publication: *Human Rights Abuses in a War against Civilians* (AI, September 1995, 27pp)

SOUTH AFRICA

The attorney-general of Kwa-Zulu Natal, Tim McNally, is suing the *Mail & Guardian* newspaper for R250,000 (US$ 68,000) over reports published in August criticising his handling of investigations into the activities of hit squads.

An inquest into the 1985 murders of the 'Craddock Four' anti-apartheid activists has revealed the destruction of 'tens of thousands' of classified documents. It is thought that the destruction of secret files began shortly after the African National Congress (ANC) was unbanned in 1990. (*Guardian*)

A recently released report from the Independent Broadcasting Authority (IBA) proposes delaying the introduction of any new terrestrial channels until 1998. This gives satellite television stations over two years to establish themselves with only limited competition. (*Mail & Guardian*)

Tshepo Ranto, president of the National Community Media Forum, has accused the commercial press of failing to keep to their promises of assisting the community press, and only paying lip service to media diversity. The criticism came after expected subsidies from commercial papers to smaller independent publications failed to materialise. (*Southern Africa Report*)

The Central News Agency (CNA), South Africa's largest book and magazine retail chain, has said it intends to reduce the number of pornographic magazines that it carries. Sixty pornographic magazines have appeared since the former National Party government's censorship laws were repealed. CNA has said it will sell only seven of them. The Freedom of Expression Institute (FXI) has congratulated CNA on its decision, arguing that pornography should be regulated at the market-place, and not by the government. (*Southern Africa Report*)

SOUTH KOREA

On 16 September riot police in Seoul fired tear gas at a crowd of 1,000 demonstrators protesting the government's decision not to indict former presidents Chun Doo Hwan and Roh Tae-woo for their part in the suppression of the 1980 civil uprisings. Similar skirmishes with police were reported as students mounted protests across the country on 29 September, 3 and 7 October, and demonstrators were arrested on 16 October

when they raided the offices of the Democratic Liberal Party. (Reuter, SWB)

Students Chong Min-joo and Lee Hye-jong were arrested under the National Security Law on 3 October as they returned from Korean independence rallies in North Korea. Fifty students who had gathered near the border to greet the two were detained by police. (Reuter, *Daily Telegraph*)

The trial of Pak Yong-kil (*Index* 5/1995) was cancelled on 4 October when she refused to attend. Pak, accused of violating the National Security Law, has argued that she should instead be charged under the law on South-North exchanges. (Reuter, SWB)

SRI LANKA

Government interference in the press continues (*Index* 5/1995): between 5 and 10 September police raided the offices of *Lakbima* and questioned the editor about an article accusing the government of extravagance. Police also questioned journalists at *Hiro* for four days after the paper called for the resignation of the police chief. On 12 September, following a complaint by President Kumaratunga about an article which criticised the ruling party, police searched the office of Lasantha Wickrematunga, editor of the *Sunday Leader*. (RSF)

The government imposed censorship on all military

news from 21 September, the day after an offensive in the Jaffna region. The minister for information said censorship would only be temporary, but diplomats say the ban will inhibit human rights groups working to protect civilians in Jaffna. On 26 September restrictions were relaxed on foreign media reports of the civil war. This followed claims by French doctors working in the Jaffna peninsula that 68 civilians, including 34 children, were killed in attacks by government forces on 21 and 22 September. On 19 October Wimal Wickremasinghe, the editor of the weekly *Janajaya* and a former United National Party minister, filed a suit against the restrictions in the Supreme Court, charging 'violation of a fundamental right'. (Reuter)

Bandula Padmakumara, editor of *Lakbima*, Upali Tennakoon, editor-in-chief of *Divaina*, and other newspaper editors formed an Editors' Guild on 16 October to lobby the government on issues including the lifting of military censorship. (Reuter)

BBC correspondent George Arney was wounded in crossfire on 20 October as government forces fired on Tamil guerrillas who were attacking the Orugodawatta oil and gas installation near Colombo. (Reuter)

Recent publication: *Correspondence with the Liberation Tigers of Tamil Eelam on Human Rights Abuses* (AI, September 1995, 10pp)

SUDAN

Hassan el-Tourabi, the country's de facto ruler, told his supporters on 17 September, after five days of demonstrations in Khartoum, to arm themselves in preparation for a confrontation with General Omar al-Bashir's regime. The demonstrations were the largest street protests to have taken place in Sudan since the military government came to power in 1989. They appear to have been sparked off by the arrest of 23 students and teachers on 2 September and widespread discontent with the economic situation. El-Tourabi's National Islamic Front is blamed for the shocking deterioration of the economy. The authorities also announced on 17 September that the students who had been arrested during the riots would be released, but made no mention of those arrested before the demonstrations. (*Observer*, AI, Reuter)

Members of Sudan's parliament called on thousands of Ethiopian and Eritrean refugees to return home on 11 October, in order to clear jobs and housing for the 300,000 Sudanese recently ordered to leave Libya. (Reuter)

Recent publication: *Monitoring Human Rights* (AI, October 1995, 9pp)

SWITZERLAND

On 12 September the Swiss Bankers' Association announced that it has discovered US$34 million in dormant accounts that may belong to Holocaust victims or their descendants. The decision by Swiss banks to acknowledge the existence of such accounts and to open an office to assist claimants in tracking down lost family assets was triggered by a wave of criticism in the Swiss media about the role played by Swiss banks during the Nazi period in Germany. Israel Singer, general secretary of the World Jewish Congress, warned that much of the wealth was also deposited by Nazis who confiscated it from their victims. (*International Herald Tribune*)

SYRIA

Eight journalists remain in detention: Rida Haddad, columnist with Ba'ath Party daily *Tishrin*, sentenced to eight years' imprisonment in June 1993; Isma'il al-Hadjje, sentenced to 15 years' imprisonment in June 1994; Faysal Allush, sentenced to 15 years' imprisonment for membership of the Party for Communist Action (PCA); Samir al-Hassan, Palestinian journalist with *al Asifa* and editor of *Fatah al-Intifada* magazine, sentenced in June 1994 to 15 years' imprisonment for membership of the PCA; Anwar Bader, journalist with state radio and television, arrested in 1986 and sentenced to 12 years' imprisonment in March 1994; Jadi Nawfal, sentenced to five years' imprisonment in 1992 for disseminating false information; Nizar Nayyuf, journalist and member of the banned Committee for the Defence of Democratic Freedoms and Human Rights

(CDF), sentenced to 10 years' imprisonment; and Salama George Kila, journalist with *al Wahda* and *Dirasat Arabia*, charged with membership of the CDF. (RSF)

TANZANIA

Political parties - including the ruling CCM party - have threatened to boycott the forthcoming elections because of the design of the ballot papers. They claim that the photographs of the vice-presidential candidates are confusing. On 17 October the head of the National Electoral Commission, Lewis Makame, dismissed the objections as baseless and said that they were a typical example of election fever and the panicking of political parties in the run-up to election day. (Reuter)

Police tear-gassed an opposition party rally on 15 October, resulting in a stampede which left 27 people injured. They fired gas canisters after asking the organisers of the opposition Civic United Front (CUF) to disperse in favour of another rally nearby organised by supporters of President Salmin Amour. (Reuter)

THAILAND

On 19 October the foreign minister, Kasem Kasensri, said that restrictions to the issuing of new visas for Australian journalists and the stricter scrutiny of other Australian requests for long-term visas would be dropped. The restrictions were imposed after

a cartoon appeared in the Melbourne *Age* in December 1994, showing the king giving a convicted Australian drug trafficker a pardon on his birthday. (Reuter)

TIBET

A heavy police presence was reported in Lhasa during the 30th anniversary of the establishment of the Tibet Autonomous Region. Supporters of the pro-independence movement were detained, including Buddhist monk Bado Losang Lekstok, who was previously arrested in late August for chanting independence slogans. Monks and nuns were barred entry to the city, bus services were curtailed, and only Tibetans who had been issued with photo identity cards were allowed to attend preliminary events. (Reuter)

TURKEY

Ismet Celikaslan, a member of the Mersin branch of HADEP (People's Democracy Party), was detained in Mersin on 27 September, after appearing on the Kurdish-owned satellite channel *MedTV*, which broadcasts to Turkey from outside the country. She talked about her daughter, Leman Celikaslan, who alleged that she was repeatedly raped while in police custody in Ankara in July. Celikaslan has been denied access to her lawyer. (AI)

On 27 September the Norwegian Authors' Union awarded Turkish author Ismail Beşikçi (*Index* 1/1983,

6/1990, 3/1994, 1/1995) its annual Freedom of Expression Prize. Beşikçi who has been sentenced to more than 70 years' imprisonment and who had 27 of his 31 books banned, was not permitted by the Turkish authorities to travel to Norway to receive the prize. (Norwegian Forum for Freedom of Expression)

Kurdish writer Recep Marasli (*Index* 1&2/1994, 4&5/1994) was sentenced to two years in prison on 28 September. Marasli was found guilty under article 8 of the Anti-Terror Law (spreading 'separatist propaganda') for writing about the Kurdish rebel movement. He faces a further 27 cases for articles or speeches he has made about the Kurdish struggle for autonomy or independence. Marasli, who has been in and out of prison since 1971, suffers from brain and nervous disorders and his supporters say he cannot get proper treatment from the Istanbul prison. (Reuter)

On 28 September publisher Ayse Zarakolu was sentenced to five months in prison in connection with the book *Birakuji: the Kurdish Civil War*. She is already serving a two-year prison sentence for publishing *The Armenian Taboo* by French author Yves Ternon (*Index* 4/1995). (PEN)

Necmiye Arslanoglu (*Index* 3/1995), Emin Arslanoglu and Mevlut Bozkur, three Kurdish journalists whose trial was supposed to start on 3 October, were released on that date by Diyarbakir State Security Court. No date was

'It's always a pleasure to see an objective journalist...'

set for their trial, effectively dropping all charges. (Kurdistan Information Centre)

Haluk Gerger (*Index* 1/1995, 5/1995) was not released from detention on expiry of his sentence on 23 September, owing to his refusal to pay a fine that accompanied his prison sentence. On 20 October Gerger was sentenced to another 20 months in prison and ordered to pay another fine for an article published in the now-defunct pro-Kurdish newspaper *Özgür Gündem* (Free Agenda). (PEN)

On the night of 7-8 October Istanbul anti-terror police arrested four journalists and three staff of the left-wing weekly *Atilim*. Journalists Sultan Secik, Bayram Namaz, Ramanzan Basci and Metin

Yesil, *Atilim* owner Aslan Yucesan, secretary Sevil Yesil and newspaper vendor Ferahmuz Lule, were all arrested in their homes. According to police, six of them were detained for questioning at the anti-terror department of Istanbul security headquarters. Yesil and Secik reportedly needed hospital treatment after being beaten in detention. In early September Yesil had been beaten by police while covering a demonstration in Istanbul. On 5 September Eylem Semint, the paper's editor-in-chief, was arrested by the Istanbul State Security Court and is currently being prosecuted under the Anti-Terror Law. *Atilim* has repeatedly been seized since it began publishing in October 1994. (RSF)

On 12 October Aliz Marcus,

Istanbul correspondent for Reuter, appeared before the Istanbul State Security Court on a charge of inciting racial hatred. Marcus is charged in connection with a dispatch she wrote, which was translated into Turkish and reprinted in the now-defunct pro-Kurdish daily *Özgür Ülke* (Free Country). (RSF)

Over the past several months, Turkish authorities have effectively banned foreign journalists from Iraqi Kurdistan, the autonomous area of northern Iraq occupied by Turkish forces. Officially, foreign journalists are allowed into the region if they obtain permission from the Turkish embassy in their home country. However, under a Ministry of Foreign Affairs decree, foreign journalists can only enter the area if they also possess a visa from the Iraqi

REPORTERS SANS FRONTIÈRES

authorities, which is almost impossible to obtain. Only accredited correspondents in Turkey and Turkish journalists can enter the region through one point of entry, the Habur border crossing. (RSF)

Recent publication: *Unfulfilled Promise of Reform* (AI, September 1995, 16pp)

UNITED KINGDOM

Nuclear Electric failed to warn local people put at risk by a potentially catastrophic accident in one of its nuclear reactors in Wylfa, and told them nothing about it until days after the danger was over. The company was fined £250,000 (US$400,000) in

early September for 'blatant violation' of safety rules after the accident on 31 July 1993. (*Independent*)

At the end of September the BBC set up an internal unit to monitor 'intimidatory and abusive behaviour' by politicians and their spin doctors seeking to influence the news agenda in the run-up to the general election. Reporters and producers working at Westminster and on current affairs programmes like *Newsnight* and *Today* were told to report attempts where 'undue pressure' was being brought to bear. (*Independent*)

On 6 October the Prince of Wales secured a worldwide ban on a book written by his

former housekeeper Wendy Berry. *Diary of a Housekeeper* records intimate details of the royal household and was written in breach of her employment contract, which includes a worldwide undertaking in perpetuity not to discuss her time at the house. A judge ruled that any profits from the book, which has already been published in the USA and Canada, are to be handed over to the Prince, along with all originals and copies of any diaries or manuscripts containing details concerning any members of the royal family, their guests or visitors. (*Times*)

The Scottish Prison Officers' Association failed on 11 October in its bid to obtain an interim ban on a BBC

REPORTERS SANS FRONTIÈRES

Index congratulates Reporters Sans Frontières on their tenth anniversary, 1985-1995

documentary that contains allegations of violent assaults committed by prison officers against inmates at Barlinnie prison in 1994. (*Guardian*)

USA

On 15 September Mumia Abu-Jamal (*Index* 2/1995, 4/1995, 5/1995) was denied a retrial by Judge Albert Sabo, the judge who sentenced him to death in 1982. Abu-Jamal's lawyers are to appeal the decision. The European Parliament called on the Pennsylvania authorities to review Abu-Jamal's sentence on 21 September. (PEN)

On the advice of the attorney-general and the director of the FBI, the *Washington Post* and the *New York Times* agreed to print a 35,000-word tract entitled *Industrial Society and Its Future*, written by the notorious Unabomber on 19 September. In return, the bomber promised to cease the attacks that he has been carrying out for the past 17 years, mainly on technological and industrial targets, in which three people have been killed and 23 injured. (*Financial Times, Independent*)

On 2 October the Supreme Court unanimously upheld a ruling of the New Jersey Supreme Court that shopping malls must allow protesters to hand out leaflets on controversial social issues. A New Jersey mall owner had appealed to the court on the basis that the ruling required the mall to furnish a valuable part of its private property to protest groups espousing causes that the mall did not endorse. (Reuter)

In early October, the Court of Appeals upheld the government's right to ban indecent programming between the hours of 6am and 10pm. The court ruled that there is a 'compelling interest' in restricting the broadcast of 'language or material that... depicts or describes, in terms patently offensive as measured by contemporary community standards... sexual or excretory activities or organs'. In two previous cases, courts have ruled the restrictions unconstitutional. (*Variety*)

On 6 October President Clinton announced the lifting of the 25-year ban on Cuban news bureaus operating in the USA, and removed restrictions on US journalists operating out of Cuba. (CPJ)

The Institute of Electrical and Electronics Engineers urged Congress on 19 October that Internet-filtering technology, rather than government controls on the information flow, is the best way to protect children from electronic pornography. It has pledged that US engineers will devote their energies to developing the relevant technology. (PR Newswire)

On 19 October Lee Brown, head of the Office of National Drug Control Policy, condemned a new Capricorn Records release called *Hempilation* as liable to lead 'the young and innocent' into drug use. The record features 17 artists singing such songs as 'Who's Got the Herb?' and 'Legalize it'. Brown said he does not advocate government censorship but that 'some self-regulation and self-monitoring are not too much to expect.' (Reuter)

On 20 October the Senate debated a controversial proposal to amend the Constitution so as to extend the right to worship and express religious beliefs in public. Supporters of the proposal say the Supreme Court's rulings on the subject have restricted the right of students to pray and hold religious meetings in schools. Opponents fear, however, that any change to the First Amendment would weaken the separation of church and state. (Reuter)

Business Week publishers McGraw-Hill filed a brief in the Court of Appeals on 23 October, alleging prior restraint by District Judge John Feikens. In September Feikens issued a restraining order against *Business Week*, delaying for three weeks publication of an article about a pending compensation suit brought by Procter & Gamble against Bankers Trust New York. The case is due to be heard on 6 December. (Reuter)

The broad anti-terrorist legislation proposed in the wake of the Oklahoma City bomb (*Index* 3/1995) appears to have stalled in Congress, despite its speedy progress through the Senate. A coalition of libertarian Representatives from both parties, alarmed by the wide-ranging new powers the bill gives to the police and the FBI, have blocked its introduction into the House this autumn. (*International Herald Tribune*)

VIETNAM

On 13 October the Ministry for Culture and Information announced its intention to crack down on foreign organisations or individuals who hold media briefings without seeking permission at least 12 hours in advance. The statement came after the Vietnam Brewery Ltd held a press conference without permission for which it was fined US$900. (SWB)

The state telecommunications authority announced plans on 14 October to attempt to control Internet supply to Vietnam by installing a high-capacity line between Vietnam and the US. A spokesman for the Vietnam Data Communication Company said: 'The Internet must be controlled, not only for technical and security reasons, but from the cultural aspect. Abroad there are some organisations who don't like our state. From abroad they can send information.' (*Financial Times*)

ZAIRE

Nine demonstrators were killed and 23 injured during an opposition demonstration on 29 July. Security forces used firearms to disperse the demonstration being held by the Parti Lumbiste Unifié

(PALU). They were protesting against the two-year postponement of elections that had been scheduled for July. (AI)

Recent publication: *Zairian Human Rights Activists under Threat* (AI, September 1995, 5pp)

ZAMBIA

The Zambian Union of Journalists (ZUJ) has accused the government of trying to muzzle the press, following the suspension of the acting managing editor of the *Times of Zambia*, Arthur Simuchoba. Simuchoba was suspended in September, pending an investigation into alleged financial mismanagement. Although it is state-owned, the *Times* is relatively outspoken in its criticism of the government. (MISA)

Three journalists from the *Post* newspaper — Bright Mwape, Goliath Mungonge and Nkonkomalimba Kafunda — were detained for several hours on 22 September after the judge in the ongoing defamation case against the paper (*Index* 5/1995) cancelled their bail. The judge ruled that the *Post*'s editor, Fred M'membe, had broken bail regulations by travelling to Germany, and that the defence lawyers were prolonging the case unnecessarily. It has so far been adjourned 20 times. The detention order was immediately overturned by the High Court. On 7 October, M'membe received MISA's Press Freedom Award for 1995. (MISA)

General publication: *1995 Directory of Persecuted Scientists, Engineers and Health Professionals* (American Association for the Advancement of Science, August 1995, 220pp); *Concerns in Europe, January-June 1995* (AI, September 1995, 59pp); *Blinding Laser Weapons — the Need to Ban a Cruel and Inhumane Weapon* (HRW/Arms Project, September 1995, 54pp); *The Death Penalty — No Solution to Illicit Drugs* (AI, October 1995, 46pp); *Double Jeopardy: Homophobic Attacks on the Press 1990-1995* (CPJ, October 1995)

***

Compiled by: Anna Feldman, Jason Garner, Kate Thal (Africa); Nathalie de Broglio, Dionne King (Americas); Nicholas McAulay, Saul Venit, Sarah Smith (Asia); Laura Bruni, Robert Horvath, Robin Jones, Oleg Pamfilov, Vera Rich (eastern Europe and CIS); Michaela Becker, Philippa Nugent (Middle East); Jamie McLeish, Predrag Zivkovic (western Europe)

***

Contributors

John Baxter is a writer on film and media based in Paris. He has published biographies of Federico Fellini and Luis Buñuel. His biography of Steven Spielberg (Harper Collins) will appear in 1996.

Kathryn Bigelow's latest film is *Strange Days*; others include *Near Dark, Blue Steel* and *Point Break*.

John Boorman's films include *Point Blank, Hell in the Pacific, Deliverance, The Emerald Forest, Hope and Glory* and, in 1995, *Beyond Rangoon*.

Aida Bortnik is an author of television scripts and plays, a journalist and critic. *The Official Version* is her seventh co-written screenplay.

Nouri Bouzid, a member of a left-wing group in Tunisia, spent six years in prison.

Ian Buruma is a writer living in London. His most recent book is *The Wages of Guilt* (Jonathan Cape, 1994).

Arthur C Clarke's bestselling novels include *Rendezvous with Rama, Childhood's End, The Ghost from the Grand Banks, The Hammer of God* and *2001*, the novel from the ground-breaking film directed by Stanley Kubrick. He now lives in Sri Lanka.

Constantin Costa-Gavras, born in Greece in 1933, is now a naturalised Frenchman living in Paris. His political thrillers include *Z, The Confession, Missing* and *Betrayed*.

Milos Forman has been a US citizen since 1975. His Czech-language films include *Loves of a Blond* and *The Firemen's Ball*. Notable among his English-language films are *Taking Off, One Flew Over the Cuckoo's Nest, Amadeus* and *Valmont*.

Jonathan Foreman is currently working on a biography of his father, Carl Foreman.

Philip French was a writer-producer with BBC Radio for 30 years and has been film critic of the *Observer* since 1977. He was a founding sponsor of the Society for the Defence of Literature and the Arts. His books include *The Age of Austerity 1945-51, The Movie Moguls, Westerns* and monographs on Bergman's *Wild Strawberries* and Louis Malle.

Haile Gerima left Ethiopia for the US in 1967. He is a radical film-maker and Professor of Film at Howard University, Washington. His feature film *Harvest: 3000 Years* (1976) established him as an exponent of African and Third World Cinema.

Peter Hames lectures in Film and Media Studies at Staffordsire University, UK, and recently edited *Dark Alchemy: The Films of Jan Švankmajer* (Flicks Books).

Marjorie Heins has been director and staff counsel of the American Civil Liberties Union Arts Censorship Project since its inception in 1991; also a board member of the US-based Feminists for Free Expression. Her most recent book, on which her article is based, is *Sex, Sin, and Blasphemy: A Guide to America's Censorship Wars* (New Press, 1993).

Shahrukh Husain collaborated on the script of *In Custody*, Ismail Merchant's directorial feature debut. Her latest book is *Women Who Wear the Breeches (Virago, 1995)*.

Sheila Johnston is a film critic and feature writer for the London *Independent*.

Mark Kermode is a freelance writer and broadcaster on film. His forthcoming book, *The Fear of God,* is on *The Exorcist*.

Krzysztof Kieślowski is best known for his *Dekalog,* originally made for Polish television, and for the trilogy *Three Colours Blue, White* and *Red*.

Ken Loach has directed many films for cinema and television, including *Poor Cow, Kes, Raining Stones, Ladybird Ladybird* and *Hidden Agenda*. His latest film, *Land and Freedom*, is about the Spanish Civil War.

Kevin Macdonald is a documentary film-maker. His biography of his grandfather *Emeric*

Pressburger: The Life and Death of a Screenwriter (Faber & Faber) appeared last year; *Imagining Reality: The Faber Book of the Documentary*, edited with Mark Cousins, will be published in September 1996.

Jiří Menzel's films include the Oscar-winning *Closely Observed Trains* and *Larks on a String*. *The Life and Extraordinary Adventures of Private Ivan Chonkin* opened in 1995.

Ismail Merchant has collaborated as producer on many films with James Ivory and Ruth Praba Jhabvala, including *Shakespeare Wallah*, *Heat and Dust* and *A Room with a View*. His current film is called *Surviving Picasso*. He has also directed his own films.

Jane Mills, a documentary film-maker and author, joined the Australian Film, Television & Radio School as Head of Screen Studies in 1995. Her books include: *The Bloomsbury Guide to Erotic Literature* (Bloomsbury), *Sexwords* (Penguin) and *Womanwords* (Virago).

Julian Petley heads Communication and Information Studies at Brunel University, UK.

Nadezhda Pokornaya is a Russian scriptwriter. Her feature, *In Thee I Trust*, won prizes at Film Festivals in Japan, Switzerland, Canada and Russia.

Roman Polanski studied at the Lodz Film School and left Poland after the international success of his first feature, *Knife in the Water* (1962). He subsequently worked in Britain, France and the USA. His many English-language movies include *Repulsion*, *Cul de Sac*, *Rosemary's Baby*, *Chinatown*, *Tess*, and *Death and the Maiden*. He now lives in Paris.

Tony Rayns is a London-based film-maker, critic, lecturer and festival programmer. He co-organised the world's first historical retrospective of Chinese cinema at London's National Film Theatre in 1980.

Sally Sampson was for 10 years a part-time examiner for the British Board of Film Classification from which she resigned in 1992. She has translated books on Simone Signoret and Elia Kazan from the French, and co-edited *The Oxford Book of Ages*.

John Sayles, actor, author and director, lives in Hoboken, New Jersey. His films include *The Return of the Secaucus Seven*, *Matewan*, *Eight Men Out* and *City of Hope*.

Quentin Tarantino was born in Tennessee and grew up in Southern California. Before writing and directing *Reservoir Dogs* and *Pulp Fiction*, he wrote the original scripts for *True Romance* and *Natural Born Killers*.

Bertrand Tavernier's films include *The Watchmaker*, *Sunday in the Country*, *Round Midnight*, *Life and Nothing But*, *L 627* and, most recently, *The Bait* (*L'Appât*).

Andrzej Wajda trained at the Lodz Film School, Poland. His best-known films are the war trilogy *A Generation*, *Kanal* and *Ashes and Diamonds*, and the political chronicles *Man of Marble* and *Man of Iron*, made at the time of Solidarity. He has just finished *Holy Week* and started work on a new film provisionally called *Miss Nobody*.

John Waters was born in Baltimore. His best known underground movies are *Pink Flamingos*, *Multiple Maniacs* and *Female Trouble*; mainstream titles include *Hairspray*, *Cry Baby* and *Serial Mom*. He is working on a new film, *Cecil B Demented*.

Bernard Williams is White's Professor of Moral Philosophy at the University of Oxford and Deutsch Professor of Philosophy at the University of California, Berkeley. His many publications include *Shame and Necessity* (University of California Press); *Making Sense of Humanity* (Cambridge University Press) was published this year.

Geoffrey Wood was a part-time examiner at the BBFC from 1983-1994. For many years a teacher and academic, he is now director of the Central and Eastern European Programme at the Hansard Society for Parliamentary Government.

Tian Zhuangzhuang's best-known films are *Horse Thief* and *The Blue Kite*. He now works as a producer in China. ❏